The Play of the Text

The Play
of the Text

Max Jacob's
Le Cornet à dés

Sydney Lévy

with translations of selected
poems and prose
from *Le Cornet à dés*
by
Judith Morganroth Schneider

The University of Wisconsin Press

Published 1981

The University of Wisconsin Press
114 North Murray Street
Madison, Wisconsin 53715

The University of Wisconsin Press, Ltd.
1 Gower Street
London WC1E 6HA, England

First printing

Printed in the United States of America

For LC CIP information see the colophon

ISBN 0-299-08510-4

Poems from Max Jacob's *Le Cornet à dés*, copyright 1945 by Editions Gallimard
are included by permission of Editions Gallimard.

Publication of this book has been made possible in part by a grant from the
Andrew W. Mellon Foundation.

for Judi

Quand on fait un tableau, à chaque touche, il change tout entier, il tourne comme un cylindre et c'est presque interminable. Quand il cesse de tourner, c'est qu'il est fini. Mon dernier représentait une tour de Babel en chandelles allumées.

Max Jacob, *Le Cornet à dés*

Des coups de dés s'isolent les uns des autres. Rien ne les rassemble en un *tout*. Le tout est la nécessité. Les dés sont libres.

Georges Bataille, *L'Expérience intérieure*

Soit un certain nombre de cubes légers recouverts d'un matériau magnétique, et caractérisé par la polarisation opposée des deux paires des trois côtés qui se joignent en deux coins opposés. On place les cubes dans une boîte que l'on ferme et que l'on agite. Sous l'effet de l'agitation, les cubes s'associent selon une architecture aléatoire (fantaisiste) et stable. A chaque nouvelle agitation, des cubes rentrent dans le système et le complètent, jusqu'à ce que la totalité des cubes constitue une unité originale, imprévisible au départ en tant que telle, ordonnée et organisée à la fois.

Edgar Morin, *La Méthode I, La nature de la nature*

Contents

Acknowledgments

Renée Riese Hubert and Judd Hubert are at the origin of this study: it is they who taught me to read poetry. For years Michel Pierssens has served as a reliable sounding board (when I get the chance to see him). I also owe much to Alfred Glauser, who took the time to read the manuscript through its various stages, and to Neal Oxenhandler, whose criticism and suggestions were invaluable. I am also extremely grateful to Carl R. Lovitt, who translated with considerable patience a substantial portion of my original manuscript, which has subsequently undergone revision. Many thanks also go to Yvonne Schofer and Elizabeth Evanson of the University of Wisconsin Press staff for editing the manuscript. Finally, I would like to thank Judith Morganroth Schneider for having translated the poems quoted as well as the important "1916 Preface" (first appearing in the 1923 edition published by Stock) and "Brief Historical Account of *The Dice Cup*" (1943), which have both become standard inclusions in the editions of *Le Cornet à dés*. Her contribution, I hope, will give an entirely new character to this volume by presenting to an English-speaking audience an important selection of texts by Max Jacob. I take this opportunity to note that her translations are not literal, on the one hand, nor, on the other, are they intended to propitiate my readings of the poems; instead, they are independent translations and should stand on their own. I therefore found it appropriate to quote the French version, rather than the English, in my text and to provide a double numerical reference. The first number, in italics, refers to the poem number in the translations located at the end of this volume, where the poems are ordered in the sequence in which they appear in *Le Cornet à dés* (1917; rpt. Paris: Gallimard, Collection "Poésie/Gallimard," 1967). The second reference gives the page number on which the poem appears in the Gallimard edition.

Early versions of Chapters 3 and 4 appeared in *Sub-Stance*, no. 4 (1972), pp. 27–44. Chapter 7 appeared in *Folio*, no. 4 (Oct. 1976), pp. 5–14, and parts of Chapter 5 were read at the Max Jacob Special Session, MLA Convention, 1976. Chapter 8 as well as considerable revisions were written in 1977–78 while I was a Fellow at the Camargo Foundation in Cassis, supported by a grant from the Graduate School Research Committee, University of Wisconsin–Madison.

The Play of the Text

1

MARGINS

L'art est un jeu. Tant pis pour
celui qui s'en fait un devoir.
—Max Jacob, *La Défense de Tartufe*

Until very recently, nearly every article or book written about Max Jacob has attempted to situate him within certain modern—and some not so modern—tendencies. His
writing has been described as fantastical, lyrical, classical,
modern, serious, whimsical; he has been described as a cubist, a proto-surrealist, a mystic, a martyr. . . . This persisting
effort to classify him, sixty years after the publication of his
Cornet à dés (1917) and more than thirty years following his
tragic death in a concentration camp (1944), is symptomatic
of the mystery that still surrounds him. We have only to compare his case with that of his contemporaries, Apollinaire or
Valéry, both of whom are sufficiently well-known to spare
their critics the necessity of identifying them, even in works
destined for an English-speaking audience. Yet the problem
faced in any presentation of Max Jacob is not that he is unknown; the problem lies instead in the effusive and multifac-
eted image he presented of himself. His name recurs without
fail in treatises on the history of modern music and art, in
studies of the avant-garde between the two wars, and in books
on modern poetry. Yet his name is consistently accorded a
marginal status. Discussions of Picasso's early years as a struggling artist in Paris, for example, invariably contain references to Max Jacob as a close friend and neighbor of the artist
in Montmartre. In the same circle of artists were Guillaume
Apollinaire, André Salmon, Paul Reverdy, Juan Gris, and

numerous others who have since become famous and who, unlike Max Jacob, have been attributed clearly defined identities.

In fact, Max Jacob never identified himself in a permanent fashion with any group, movement, or personality. During his entire life he always took a special interest in any young writer who wrote to him; having prepared an astrological chart on the writer, Max Jacob would enter into an energetic correspondence with him or her. This accounts for the fact that his name frequently reoccurs in discussions of Michel Leiris, Jean Cocteau, Marcel Jouhandeau, Edmond Jabès, or Gertrude Stein, to name but a few and to indicate the variety of those he knew and with whom he corresponded. Even a detailed study of a single period of his life would yield evidence of his marginality: during his Montmartre phase, penniless, he worked at a variety of jobs—journalist, piano teacher, tutor, salesman, janitor, expert in horoscopy, art critic, and others. Of course, he also worked closely with his friends and with them discussed literature and art day and night, but it is they who were to begin to formulate the theoretical bases of *art nouveau* and cubism, the two movements which have had the greatest impact on our esthetic perception. Owing to his playful personality, Max Jacob was generally treated as the clown of the clan, a man given to practical jokes and preoccupied with wordplay.

Efforts to classify him among those who have been called cubist writers would also fail. Not that his work is devoid of reference to cubism. In *Le Cornet à dés* alone, there are numerous allusions to that movement, as in "Père Double Sphère" (*12l*; p. 67)[1] and "Cubisme et soleil noyés" (*23*; p. 88), and in the line "nous n'avons plus de peinture" (*26*; p. 95), which is an implied reference to the controversy surrounding the emergence of cubist painting. Nevertheless, for

---

1. In these parenthetical citations, the numbers in italic type refer to the translated poems at the end of this volume, ordered in the sequence in which they appear in the Gallimard edition; page numbers refer to that edition: *Le Cornet à dés* (1917; rpt. Paris: Gallimard, Collection "Poésie/Gallimard," 1967).

reasons to be examined, cubism never became as well established in literature as it did in painting. If Max Jacob is marginal with regard to cubism as a movement, he is also marginal with regard to surrealism, which did become established in both literature and art. Although his work features techniques that were later considered fundamental to surrealism (an emphasis upon dreams and language, for example), Max Jacob was never admitted to the group and was even slandered by André Breton.

His marginality is also due to what has been termed the protean quality of his work: novels, essays, tearful or mocking letters, children's stories (his first publication, which, incidentally, earned him a literary award), poems signed Morven le Gaëlique (inspired by his native Brittany), still other poems whose blatant punning and playfulness marked an apparent break with the poetic tradition of the turn of the century.

If we wish to single out an event that clearly summarizes his marginality, we can cite his conversion to Roman Catholicism and its consequences. A Jew by birth, he had a vision of Christ one day in his room; perhaps typically he had another vision at the movies. These experiences led him to seek someone to baptize him, someone, in other words, who would take his new faith seriously, who would help eliminate his marginality and introduce him into an established order; it took him five years to find that person. Picasso served as his godfather, a sure sign that bohemianism, art, and Montmartre had not been discarded with his conversion. True, he was then writing one meditation per day, but these meditations are for the most part indistinguishable from certain poems in the *Cornet* in terms of their humor and verbal acrobatics. There is no doubt that he fervently believed in his new faith, but it did not affect his personality or his art. The result was that Christianity tolerated his presence in its midst with difficulty: numerous are the testimonies that cast doubts on his conversion. At the same time, his marginality with regard to the avant-garde was actually reinforced because of his new beliefs—reinforced to such an extent that he left Paris (a concrete sign

of his marginality) and withdrew to the Abbaye de Saint-Be-
noît-sur-Loire, where he continued to meditate, to write, and
to paint the gouaches that earned him enough to buy his ciga-
rettes and stamps. He went back to Paris only once for any
lengthy period before returning definitively to Saint-Benoît,
where he was seized by the Gestapo in 1944.

Far from wanting to repress this marginality in order to tip
the balance in favor of his participation in some group or
other, as has been done[2]—far from wanting to shelve him
somewhere, I propose to take the case of Max Jacob literally:
to exploit this very marginality, to confront it and multiply it.
In other words, rather than considering Max Jacob a failed
cubist, a failed surrealist, a failed Jew, or a failure of any sort,
I propose to view his marginality as a *front*, a narrow
boundary that belongs to none of the systems it separates yet
incorporates them all, something which contains signs of each
system, which announces the new yet retains traces of the old.
It is interesting to note, incidentally, that several literary figures, such as Georges Bataille, Antonin Artaud, Raymond
Queneau, and Michel Leiris, who were rejected by the surrealists and whose writing had remained unread and in a certain sense unreadable, are being discovered today as the authors of an entirely new writing. It is as if, in addition to the
movements that proclaimed themselves so loudly in the early
part of this century, there were others, silent and parallel,
imperceptible and diffuse, that are only today beginning to
blossom. And Max Jacob perhaps belongs to that silence.
Now, after a half century of literature, we may at last be permitted to read Max Jacob, to recognize that he is entering

2. Note particularly a book entitled *Max Jacob au sérieux* (Rodez: Subervie,
1958), written by one of his friends, Jean Rousselot, ostensibly in response to
an article published as an introduction to Jacob's correspondence which
opened with the question of whether the time had come to take Max Jacob
seriously (*Correspondance I: Quimper-Paris, 1876–1921*, ed. François Garnier,
Paris: Éditions de Paris, 1953). His turbulent and multidimensional existence
has inspired numerous appreciations, recollections, anecdotes, and tributes—
most of which stress his life at the expense of his significant poetic achieve-
ments.

a new order, a new order which he has perhaps helped to create.[3]

In order to classify or identify Max Jacob, then, it would be insufficient to study one of his projected images or to catalog them all, or to re-create the atmosphere of the avant-garde at the beginning of the century, or even to analyze his beliefs or his explicit esthetic theories (to which I shall nevertheless make periodic references). Instead, one must first find what constitutes this new order and determine the underlying principles in Max Jacob's writing—in other words, determine what principles are in the process of being imperceptibly formulated. In this way, this study will serve as an introduction to the work of Max Jacob, not as a general overview nor as an inventory of recurring themes, but rather as an attempt to reveal the building blocks in his poetry and the relation of that poetry to a literary current that is changing and developing at an astonishing rate. Therein lies one of the premises of this study: in order to discuss an author intelligently in relation to his social or historical context, or to literary history, or even in relation to his life, one must first examine what his work does; in order to speak of it from without, one must first understand it from within.

Within Max Jacob's work we will find preoccupations in the process of formation that, from time to time, take form and

3. As an example of the rediscovery of Max Jacob, Gallimard has been reprinting his works for the past few years. The last to appear, *Le Cabinet noir* (1922), was released in paperback and was intended for wide distribution (Collection "L'Imaginaire," 1977). Two other recent books on Max Jacob should also be mentioned. One is a dissertation (a "thèse d'état") on his style: René Plantier, *L'Univers poétique de Max Jacob* (Paris: Klincksieck, 1976). The other is a biography: Robert Guiette, *La Vie de Max Jacob* (Paris: Nizet, 1976). Two books have also been recently published in the United States: Annette Thau, *Poetry and Antipoetry: A Study of Selected Aspects of Max Jacob's Poetic Style* (Chapel Hill: University of North Carolina Dept. of Romance Languages, 1976), and Judith Morganroth Schneider, *Clown at the Altar: The Religious Poetry of Max Jacob* (Chapel Hill: University of North Carolina Dept. of Romance Languages, 1978). Further evidence of this renewed interest in Max Jacob in the United States is *The Prose Poem, an International Anthology*, edited by Michael Benedict (New York: Dell, 1977), which contains more selections from Max Jacob's poetry than from that of any other poet.

emerge. Here lies the true identity of Max Jacob—in literary terms, of course: in his text and in what it does. The question of Max Jacob's identity must therefore be displaced. "Who is Max Jacob?" must be replaced by "What did Max Jacob do?" In a sense, the answer to the latter question will constitute this study in its entirety; it will also, obliquely, answer the former.

As will soon be apparent, this study of Max Jacob derives from observations of movements, of fluxes and entities almost imperceptible at the surface of the text. Often ambiguous and contradictory, they were probably the object of conscious or subliminal preoccupations at a given point in his life. It seemed therefore appropriate, in the interest of avoiding confusion, to choose those poems most closely gathered in time and space. I have chosen a selection of poems that Max Jacob himself gathered in what is perhaps his best-known collection: *Le Cornet à dés* (1917).

A work is always in the process of developing and changing. Literary critics are the ones who hem it in with notions or place it in preconceived categories, who in the process deny it its experimental aspects and thereby fix it for a certain time. Too long a time, in the case of Max Jacob, who lies buried beneath the labels heaped upon him. I hope that, while serving as an introduction to his work, this book will set in motion and give free play to the great machine that is his writing.

2 ⬡

The Play of the Text

A thought may be
perceived by the historian
either as order or as noise.
—Michel Serres, *La Communication*

Max Jacob's poetry neither lays foundations nor draws conclusions. It institutes little or nothing that has not already been practiced, yet practices nothing that would have been considered a poetic norm at that time. Far from being insipid, however, his poetry constitutes one of the steps in a general mutation undergone by the modern text: it is in a state of metastability and ambiguity, constantly vacillating between foundation and conclusion, swept up in a process that composes new forms refashioned out of a past. It is, in short, an *experimental* poetry in which tradition and modernity, the subject and its entropy, interpretation and its limits, are juxtaposed and compete while remaining complementary.

I will begin with an example that has frequently been commented upon in criticism of Max Jacob's work: the pun. The pun naturally derives to a certain extent from Max Jacob's playful nature, from the clownish image that he encourages; in fact, most critics have sought to explain Jacob's use of the pun on the basis of his personality. Yet, given its preponderance in his poetry, given its incidence in his so-called pedagogical writings (poetic theory, advice, letters, prefaces) as well as in his religious meditations, his novels, and his prose poems,[1] the pun cannot be dismissed as a supplement that has no fundamental impact upon the nature of his writing. Instead the pun is a phenomenon, a symptom in the strongest sense, a *sign* of a systemic disturbance, of a definitive mutation in the concept of writing and in the idea of poetry. The entire system is in the process of change, of disruption, and of restructuring. Max Jacob's experimentation is not a quirk, as has been suggested, the trace of some repressed effort, but rather something much more fundamental.

Modern French writing, from Francis Ponge to Edmond Jabès, from Henri Michaux to Denis Roche, through the recent multilingual experimentations of someone like Gérard de Cortanze,[2] provides evidence of the basic importance of the pun. Of course, the pun is not always put to the same use; sometimes we find it consecrated, at other times eroticized, obscured, or exalted. Despite these thematic permutations, the pun has become an order: an essential component of what is today called "poetic." This is not to say that Max Jacob was the first to put puns to systematic use. The name of Mallarmé, the logophile,[3] quickly comes to mind; along with Rimbaud, he is Jacob's immediate predecessor. The difference, however, is that Max Jacob promoted the pun as if there could be no poetry without it,[4] just as poeticality was once equated with rhyme. Yet this manifest use of the pun is itself problematic: the pun may be repressed on the grounds that it is *noise*, a harmful quirk that represents meaning *poorly* and interferes with communication; or else it is taken literally, in all its reality, as an overt and explicit phenomenon that can-

1. According to a survey of the occurrence of puns in his works, made by René Plantier in *L'Univers poétique de Max Jacob* (Paris: Klincksieck, 1976), pp. 79–82.

2. "Le Mille-feuilles," *Sub-Stance*, no. 16 (1977), pp. 25–36.

3. "Logophilia" is a term used by Michel Pierssens, in *La tour de Babil: La Fiction du signe* (Paris: Minuit, 1977; *The Power of Babel: A Study of Logophilia*, trans. Carl R. Lovitt, London: Routledge and Kegan Paul, 1980) to characterize Mallarmé's and several other authors' obsession with language.

4. One must go back to Rabelais and the Grands Rhétoriqueurs to find anything similar.

not be overlooked, a monster invested with its own identity and instituted as a new order. "Order from noise," say information theorists, and so it is with the pun.

Max Jacob's contribution to the use of the pun in literature, however, cannot be situated within a linear evolution; chronology in this case is inverted, and the notions of sources and influences operate in reverse: Mallarmé (taken only as an example, since Lautréamont and Brisset, among others, could also be cited) introduced the modern text to the pun; Max Jacob increased and standardized its usage, but this "exteriorization"—to use one of his terms—had a negative effect: his punning was not taken seriously (his life perhaps overlapped too much with his work), it conveyed no information, it was merely "noise" in the informational as well as sensational sense. Subsequent writers, however, readopted the practice of the manifest use of the pun; and to the extent that this practice is reinstated, Max Jacob's production is informed, takes on new form, and little by little ascends the entropic ladder, in the terms of information theory, with the help of "feedback" from the modern text.

Today it is recognized that Max Jacob's text has its place and plays a role in the development of the modern text. It plays a role but it also *plays*: it is unstable and ambiguous. The example just given, his use of the pun, is not just one among others: the pun arrests attention at the signifier, and thus, by its sheer presence, prevents or obstructs so-called efficient communication. In other words, it functions as a film either without substance or as one that fashions another substance, itself ambiguous and unstable, and thereby proclaims the lack of reference and representation. The pun is therefore not only a sign of disturbance, but is itself that disturbance; it disrupts the very communication that a text is supposed to accomplish and thus puts the text into free play. This mechanism will be seen at work in each of the poems examined.

Max Jacob was aware of the play of his text when he said, in his famous "Préface de 1916": "Une œuvre d'art vaut par elle-même, et non par les confrontations qu'on peut en faire avec la réalité" (*1*; p. 23). When art cannot be confronted with reality, when, in other words, it cannot be anchored in anything outside itself and cannot be understood through a restrictive movement which directs the reader toward meaning or refers the reader to reality, art remains unbound and at play, so to speak. But here the use of an economic vocabulary reveals more of the ambiguity in Max Jacob's stand toward art and literature. Implied in his statement is another one which contradicts it: on the one hand he says that the work of art reflects nothing and is therefore worth nothing in comparison to reality, and on the other it is worth something, it has value in itself. But for there to be value, there must be a comparison with some standard, a confrontation with something held in reserve or unnamed. His statement then becomes a quasi-impossibility. He will often use a vocabulary which fails to pinpoint his meanings, and thereby suspends discourse between different systems of thought. In fact, Max Jacob struggled his entire life with problems of reflection and value, representation and referentiality.

The variety of his work, its "protean" diversity, attests to this struggle. We might, for example, group together three prose works: his *Tableau de la bourgeoisie*, which, as a *tableau*, has value as a reflection of reality or of a certain conception of that reality; his *Miroir d'astrologie*, which has value in that it provides keys; and his *Méditations religieuses*, which have value in their moral lessons. Another grouping would include his *Cornet à dés*, his *Laboratoire central*, and most of his other poetic text—all of which could readily be said to conform to his statement quoted above. Even within the same work, referential and nonreferential texts appear side by side. A poetry collection, *Ballades*, and *La Défense de Tartufe*, a montage of religious prose and verse, are examples worth noting. I will even have occasion to examine this very indecisiveness within a single text.

Again, Max Jacob was aware of being drawn in two different directions. In a letter to his mother in which he sought to explain the literary tendencies of the era, he made an implicit distinction between *Le Cornet à dés* and his other writings: "Cubism in painting is the art of working the painting itself, outside of what it represents, and according primacy to geometric construction; real life is approached only through allusion. Literary cubism does the same with literature, using reality only as a means, not as an end. Example: my *Cornet à dés* and the work of Reverdy."[5]

Max Jacob thus disengages his *Cornet* and the work of Reverdy from referentiality. He no longer speaks of his work in terms of value, but in terms of the poet's work; real life plays a role opposite to the one it plays in a referential literature: instead of being the goal, it is the means. Yet labeling this literature "cubist" is misleading: as we know today, this disengagement is characteristic of the modern text in general, and not specific to certain so-called "cubist" writers (other than Max Jacob and Reverdy, Apollinaire and André Salmon). Roland Barthes spoke of Rimbaud in such terms,[6] as did Jean Ricardou of the "new novel."[7] And even if it were possible to define cubist painting in terms of a primacy accorded to "geometric construction" (as Max Jacob suggests in the letter to his mother), it would be extremely difficult to ascribe such specificity to the literary text. Max Jacob's work does not satisfy this criterion, nor do the "calligrammes" of Apollinaire, whose ideogrammatic constructions are not always geometric and, further, strictly respect the linearity of language.[8] It could be argued, as Gerald Kamber has done, that cubist painting and literature involve similar techniques, such as simultaneity, plurality, and collage;[9] but, once again, the use of such techniques is not restricted to "cubist" writers. When Max Jacob used the epithet "literary cubism" to describe his *Cornet à dés* and the work of Reverdy, he did so first of all

5. "Letter of Max Jacob to His Mother," *Folio*, no. 9 (Oct. 1976), p. 1. my translation.

6. *Le Degré zéro de l'écriture* (Paris: Gonthier, 1953, rpt. 1964), p. 43.

7. *Pour une théorie du nouveau roman* (Paris: Seuil, 1971).

8. In comparison with what Maurice Roche does, for example. See Roche, *Compact* (Paris: Union Générale d'Éditions, 1975).

9. *Max Jacob and the Poetics of Cubism* (Baltimore: Johns Hopkins University Press, 1970). Kamber himself shows similar uses in several contemporary authors who can hardly be called "cubists," Ionesco and Prévert in particular.

because they, as well as Picasso and Apollinaire, formed a group of friends who all lived in Montmartre (Max Jacob was Picasso's neighbor in the Bateau Lavoir—a building which stood at 7, rue Ravignan and housed many a struggling artist and writer), and second because the expression "cubism in literature" was at that moment the most apt to describe a literary and artistic practice that shared the same general ideas about a modernism which was in the process of developing.

As to why cubism nevertheless failed to establish itself as solidly in literature as did surrealism, it may be that surrealism had a greater bearing on themes, meaning, and the real than on form, and that the ideas shared by the cubists were ultimately much more fundamental and were less susceptible to verbal than visual expression. One of these fundamental ideas is precisely the question of referentiality: although surrealist writings and paintings refer to the "surreal"—dreams, thoughts, an imaginary reality, etc.—rather than to the real, the fact remains that a system of reference is operative in the surrealist experience whereas, for the cubists, it is this system that begins to break down. But if cubist painting did successfully abandon reference, its literature, owing to the primordially referential nature of its medium (language), was swept up, in the process, in a tug-of-war that precluded its ever being completely free from reference.

This struggle with reference is in evidence throughout Max Jacob's writing. For the moment, I will limit myself to a single example, taken from a poem in *Le Cornet à dés*:

> Allons, tournez! tournez! vieilles pensées emprisonnées qui ne prendront jamais l'essor! le symbole qui vous sied n'est pas le galop élastique des jockeys dans la verdure, mais quelque poussiéreux bas-relief. . . .
>
> (*48*; p. 229)

There are in fact thoughts that precede language for Max Jacob, but these thoughts are imprisoned and cannot emerge. Were they to be symbolized, that is, put into language, they would take the form of either "galop élastique . . . dans la verdure" or "poussiéreux bas-relief"—two completely opposing images. Yet the reader has no way of knowing which were the original thoughts because the image communicated is the produced image: the image *fabricated* by the chosen symbol. In other words, whatever the original thought, it can exist only in the image that signifies it; if anything remains of the signified, it has, at the very least, lost its value in the poetic discourse. Signifier and signified are perceived together as an indissoluble entity; the image being an image of itself and nothing more.

This is not to say that Max Jacob's poetry has nothing to communicate; instead, it is the very possibility of communication that is challenged. If communication means the transmission of a message, independently of the form of the message, then Max Jacob's poetry does not actually communicate: the poem itself is transmitted. In other words, for Max Jacob, communication is a communication of forms, not of meanings. Evidently such effects can only be achieved from within a revised conception of poetry and from within a new system of thought.

Max Jacob's poetry reflects the transition from a closed system, where the communication of substances plays a fundamental role, to an open system, where it is no longer a question of communication but of *transformation*—what Max Jacob called "geometric constructions." The first system is characterized by a single vector where the writer directly communicates his thoughts to the page, transmitting them with the help of a binary encoding (that is a choice between *two* distinct images: "le galop élastique" *or* "poussiéreux bas-relief") in order to say what he is really thinking. The reader then makes a decoding, itself binary. Everything contained in one vessel is transmitted to the other; the writer's entropy is translated into the reader's negative entropy or information. In an open system, a multitude of small vectors enter a vessel where they are transformed, disorganized and reorganized, separated and reassembled, in order to be opposed without canceling each other out, to become complementary to each other, to mesh and form a complex network. The physical result is a locally irrecoverable expenditure of energy: *work*.

The poetic or plastic result is a poetry without foundation, meaning, or reflection, a poetry where there is no longer equivalence between the signifier and the signified, the signified and the real, or between the man and the work: an unstable poetry in perpetual motion; in effect, a *poetry in play.*

The titles alone of two of Max Jacob's collections suggest that his poetry functions as an open, complex system. *Le Laboratoire central* may be compared to what information theorists call "the black box": the poet himself, his notebook, his room, even the world are centrally located, so as to receive "inputs" from different directions, and transform or redistribute them in different directions. *Le Cornet à dés* may also be viewed in this manner: an open system which "haphazardly" combines and recombines elements introduced therein, and constantly yields different entities. Yet, whereas these two titles convey the lack of foundation (the lack of something to be said) and the possibility of aleatory recombination of a multitude of "inputs" through the subject, the very fact that Max Jacob's laboratory is *central* and that his dice cup is *unique* imposes certain limitations on the openness of his system. In totally open and highly complex systems there must be a multitude of "centers" or nodal points in which the aleatory combinations occur; the points surround themselves with networks (the combinations) that are not particular to them but shared with other points. The game of chess—which shall be discussed later—would be one example. Another example would be the experiments of the *OU. LI. PO.*[10] group in which, having established certain constraints (such as a number of fixed and limited verses, and a rigid syntactical form for these verses), they endeavored to chart vectors for each verse, to determine the points at which these vectors met, and, on the basis of these graphs, to write poems using these vectors and meeting points. Raymond Queneau succeeded in writing ten sonnets whose constraints are so efficiently designed that they permitted recombinations yielding 10^{14} sonnets.[11] Max Jacob evidently does not go this far, but it is as if

10. See *OUvroir de LIterature POtentielle* (Paris: Gallimard, 1973).
11. *Cent mille milliards de poèmes* (Paris: Gallimard, 1961).

he approached complete openness and extreme complexity while clinging to vestiges of closure and simplicity, the unique and the local. His poetry plays; it plays between the unique and the complex, but it also plays within the realm of complexity.

It should be clear that the objective of this study is not to demonstrate that Max Jacob's poetry is a game (or "nothing but a game"). My discussion will not, however, deny the playful character of his poetry: the title of his collection, *Le Cornet à dés*, and its poetic personalities, whether magician, riddler, or parodist, are sufficient evidence of this character. My goal is to show that this poetry proclaims itself to be play, but play in a new sense.

An epistemological mutation coincided with Max Jacob's writing of *Le Cornet à dés*: a mutation that betrayed itself in the birth of an avant-garde that bore several names, including surrealism, cubism, futurism, fauvism, among others, and which had general cultural impact, not only in art and literature, but also in linguistics, anthropology, philosophy, and psychology, even in biology and physics. This mutation also affects/infects what was understood by "play," and "play" begins to mean something other than what it hitherto had.[12]

12. Traditionally, play is defined as a gratuitous activity which represents a certain reality but which is different from it. In France this idea of play can be traced as far back as the seventeenth century. A remark attributed to Malherbe summarizes it well and demonstrates the association of play with poetry: "It is foolish to write verse in the hope of a reward other than one's own amusement, and a good poet is no more useful to the state than a good bowler" ("Mémoire pour la vie de Malherbe par Racan" in François de Malherbe, *Poésies* [Paris: Garnier, n.d.], p. 27; my translation). See also Jacques Ehrmann, *"Homo Ludens* Revisited," *Yale French Studies*, no. 41 (1968), pp. 32–56, for an excellent critique of this conception of play, based on several works: Johan Huizinga, *Homo Ludens: A Study of the Play Element in Culture* (1938; Eng. trans., Boston: Beacon Press, 1955), Roger Caillois, *Les Jeux et les hommes* (Paris: Gallimard, 1958; *Man, Play, and Games*, trans. Meyer Rarash, Glencoe, Ill.: Free Press, 1961), and Emile Benvéniste, "Le Jeu comme structure," *Deucalion*, no. 2 (1947), pp. 161–67. The bibliography of the concept of play is very large, since play has been considered from the point of view of many disciplines: psychoanalysis, literary criticism, linguistics, philosophy, economy, cybernetics, etc. A complete bibliography would be out of place here. I would like, however, to mention Jean Piaget, *Play, Dreams, and Imita-*

The game of chess, so extensively commented upon and repeatedly associated with the poetic text, will serve to illustrate
this new meaning.

For today's player, the chess pieces no longer represent
anything, not even "forces on a battlefield":[13] they have lost
their symbolic properties (or their "essences"[14]) and have ac-
quired a reality of their own. The queen, the knight, the
bishop are pieces of wood with different forms and functions.
The concrete pieces, their "values" (Saussure) or their "powers" (Serres) *and* their functions, establish the reality of the

---

tion in Childhood (New York: Norton, 1962), which postulates a mimetic function of play. An interesting consequence of play as imitation, based on Greg-
ory Bateson, "A Theory of Play and Fantasy," in Bateson, *Steps to an Ecology
of Mind* (New York: Ballantine, 1972), pp. 177–93, is developed by Anthony
Wilden in *System and Structure* (London: Tavistock, 1972), pp. 172–75. Wilden
argues that play is a primordial metacommunication where, for example, the
playful nip of an animal *represents* the real and injurious bite, but *is not* the
bite. It functions as a sign which says "This is play." Thus the nip is a digital
communication, whereas the bite is an analogical communication (the digital
being based on discrete elements, the analogical on a continuum). According
to Wilden, play is then a digital representation of the analogical. My argument is that *playing* is just as real as the bite—that, in short, there is a reality
of playing. For a conception of play which does not take as its starting point
imitation, the following should be mentioned: some of Huizinga's intuitions,
such as "The more we try to mark off the form we call play from other forms
apparently related to it, the more the absolute independence of the play-
concept stands out. And the segregation of play from the domain of the great
categorical antithesis does not stop here. Play lies outside the antithesis of
wisdom and folly, and equally outside those of truth and falsehood, good and
evil" (p. 6); Jacques Derrida, "Structure, Sign, Play in the Discourse of the
Human Sciences," in *The Structuralist Controversy: The Languages of Criticism
and the Criticism of Man*, ed. Richard Macksey and Eugenio Donato (Baltimore: Johns Hopkins University Press, 1970, paper ed. 1972), where play is
likened to Nietzsche's joyous affirmation; Jacques Henriot, *Le Jeu* (Paris:
Presses Universitaires de France, 1972), a stimulating study in which a difference is made between game, play, and playing; and Gilles Deleuze, *Logique du
sens* (Paris: Minuit, 1969), where play is *imagined* as an open system very close
to the one I describe here.

13. The phrase is that of W. K. Wimsatt, in "How to Compose Chess Problems and Why," *Yale French Studies*, no. 41 (1968), pp. 67–78.

14. For Wimsatt, these essences are soldiers, tanks, fighter bombers, etc.,
on the battlefield.

game.[15] Each arrangement, each configuration of the pieces, each "network" (Serres) constructs a new reality, a new order, that disrupts the preceding arrangement and will itself be destroyed by the following move. Each move is both a destroyer of order and a generator of order, producer of noise *and* order. The queen may, for example, threaten the previously secure knight who, thereby, loses his identity as an aggressor and becomes the victim: he must move or be taken. Having moved, he will in turn change the identity of another series of pieces (white and black), and so on, until checkmate suddenly, brutally concludes the game. But let us not be hasty. Let us consider any configuration, any order; it is a complete system to be studied as such: this study is itself a series of mutations between order and disorder. A simple relation is initially perceived, but any new relation derived from the first destroys it, enriches it, complicates it . . . and so on until the point of saturation, until the schema stabilizes.

This is also (or almost) the case in a modern text. The "thought" is in the image and can only be represented by the image. Each image is therefore itself and its thought (the signifier *and* the signified). The "represented" is not absent, but at the very surface of the text. Moreover, each image is caught in a complex network of relations. Reading or writing might be conceived of as a successive addition of elements (the words), each of which changes the configuration, or the context, of the poem by destroying, qualifying, complicating an order presumed established, and so on until the last word brutally ends the poem and gives it its meaning. But this is simplistic and unrealistic. One does not read a poem bit by bit, destroying and enriching the supposedly fixed meaning with the arrival of each new word. Poems, rather, are to be *re*-read. Each new reading (ideally) yields a new element, which is, furthermore, irreducible to the word—it may be a new

15. The game of chess has been used in various discussions. Ferdinand de Saussure, in *Cours de linguistique générale* (Geneva: Payot, 1931), used it to talk about the linguistic system; Michel Serres, in *Hermes I: La communication* (Paris: Minuit, 1968) used it to talk about information networks and the formation of new knowledge.

relation, a meaning overlooked, the recall of another text, or even a personal memory . . . a new element which the reader integrates and connects with the rest, and which thereby disrupts the text, and which establishes a new order until . . . but here lies the difference between the poem and the chess game, for which the exhaustion of all possibilities, and thus stability, can theoretically be attained, and the total configuration, however complex, described. The "errors" of a chess player are actually his not having "pushed his analysis" of the board far enough in a given time.[16] The poetic text, however, is "inexhaustible"; its stability can never be attained, if only because its "elements" have multiple values, while those on the chess board have single values. Furthermore, a new memory, a new element, will always arrive to destabilize and restabilize the text. In other words, if the surface of a game of chess is circumscribed, that of the text may be enlarged indefinitely through change. The text can play indefinitely. And the reader may only hope to have the aptitude to place himself at the level of this surface to observe its play.

As its title implies, *Le Cornet à dés* is a game. It has rules to its writing and rules to its reading. These rules have to be described, even if they approach Gilles Deleuze's "pure game,"[17] as they do; even if their main function is to generate more rules in the manner of Lewis Carroll, as they do. Only by first placing ourselves at the level of the "playground" can we learn the game and something about play.

16. This is the reason that a computer can play chess. The winner is the most powerful computer; in other words, the one which can exhaust the most possibilities in a given time.

17. Deleuze, *Logique du sens*, (Paris: Minuit, 1969), p. 75.

3 ⬡

Obstacles

For Max Jacob, nature, the world, or the object sought after lie beyond an impassable obstacle which rises up before him in a variety of forms. At times it is almost nothing—a thin jet of water ("une grève derrière un filet d'eau," *9*; p. 44) which separates him from and obstructs his view of the object, a holly bush ("un houx dont les feuillages laissaient voir une ville," *7*; p. 39), or else a lintel ("entre les rideaux, le linteau est une glissière," *12j*; p. 63). At other times it is as massive as a wall of bricks ("mur de briques," *12i*; p. 63), or as stifling as fog ("Brouillard, étoile d'araignée," *12g*; p. 61); it may form either an immense semicircle ("Je m'abreuve aux sources de l'atmosphère," *12a*; p. 54), or a limited one ("Ses bras devinrent tout mon horizon," *12b*; p. 55). Often the poet is himself enclosed ("Isolé, ou emprisonné, ou travaillant, Alexandre Dumas père . . . ," *11*; p. 53), cloistered in a place foreign within and without as the hotel room or prison: "Encore l'hôtel, mon ami Paul est prisonnier des Allemands" (*6*; p. 33). Imprisonment can be the consequence of not fulfilling an implicit contract, as in the case of the architect locked up for not building his cathedral (*18*; p. 81). Or, inversely, liberation may result from completing an exchange, either financial, as is the case when Olga de Berchold frees her lover (*33*; p. 112), or "esthetic," as when the poet secures his friend's release from prison (*32*; p. 108). Not only may the poet and the character be alienated, but the coveted object may also fold in upon itself and tacitly conceal its mystery: "Son ventre proéminent porte un corset d'éloignement" (*3*; p. 28).

Play: Exchange, Solitude

The isolation of the poet-player in *Le Cornet à dés* is thus extremely significant. Max Jacob's game is fundamentally solitary, a game which permits no exchange. The importance of this isolation is particularly salient when considered from the perspective of poetry in another era, the baroque period, for example, in which games were based on an exchange between adversaries. In La Fontaine's "Le Corbeau et le renard," the fox, desirous of the cheese, sets a trap for the crow in the form of an illusion, a flattering speech. It is thus the fox's creative ability which enables him to triumph over his opponent. A less evident but more significant example of exchange is found in Théophile de Viau, who is secluded in nature but who nevertheless experiences the necessity of creating around him an imaginary world which contains several characters and a complex network of exchange.[1]

Far from being in the midst of nature, Max Jacob is instead behind an obstacle which separates him from it. A certain tension results from his efforts to overcome this isolation and effect an exchange. Most often, he views the world from behind a window:

Mystère du ciel

En revenant du bal, je m'assis à la fenêtre et je contemplai le ciel: il me sembla que les nuages étaient d'immenses têtes de vieillards assis à une table et qu'on leur apportait un oiseau blanc paré de ses plumes. Un grand fleuve traversait le ciel. L'un des vieillards baissait les yeux vers moi, il allait même me parler quand l'enchantement se dissipa, laissant les pures étoiles scintillantes.

(*45*; p. 203)

"Mystère," here, takes on two overlapping meanings: in one sense, the word refers to the deep secret which the poet tries to penetrate, to something hidden by the sky's ornaments, and, in another sense, it designates a type of theatrical per-

---

1. Théophile de Viau, "La Solitude," *Oeuvres poétiques*, ed. Jeanne Streicher (1626; rpt. Geneva: Droz, 1951), pt. 1, pp. 16–23.

formance (a meaning also suggested by the words "bal," "paré," "enchantement," and even by "se dissipa," in the sense of being distracted). Therefore, it is upon returning from the ball that the ball begins, upon returning from the actual performance that the imaginary performance begins. The overlapping of the two meanings is not gratuitous; it is not simply wordplay; it serves to subvert the primary meaning of the word by making it synonymous with a performance. The profound (mystery) is made superficial (performance); the deeper meaning tends to be eroded, leaving only a perhaps senseless but nevertheless significant performance: the clouds become old men's heads seated around a table; they are brought a bird which, like the participants in the earlier ball, is adorned with its plumage—that is, inedible, unable to be incorporated. The bird does not divulge its secret to the old men, just as the "mystère" does not divulge its own to the poet. And, at the moment when a communication is nearly established with the scene (one of the old men was preparing to address him), the entire performance is wiped away, the dream evaporates, carried off by a torrent which leaves only the "étoiles scintillantes," the enigma, this one pure, having no answer, gratuitous, a new performance which obscures the first two.

The attempted exchange fails. The game is lost even before it is played. And this is so because it is inherently destined to fail: the poet seeks truth, but he constructs what he sees as a fiction, a performance, an adornment.

The imaginary force which a Théophile would exploit does not exist for Max Jacob who, alone, behind a window, is unable to give form to his game, much less win it.

Narcissus's Failure

Max Jacob ultimately intends for his window to function as a mirror which reflects his own image, a mirror which permits a narcissistic identification to occur. But, being a window rather than a mirror, it has ambivalent properties: reflecting the interior of the room (the poet), but also transparent and permitting a view of the exterior. Thus, the process of identification is destined to at least partial failure, quite unlike that of Baudelaire, who also constructs a narcissist's window. Baudelaire's window is securely closed, and it is precisely because it is closed that it does not impede the process of identification, since the closure prevents the sighting of the outside and thus permits the poet's imagination to compose a solid, idealistic image of his person.[2] Max Jacob is in search of this image of himself; he even seems to be playing the role of astrologer in "Mystère du ciel," but the transparency in this poem is interceptive and interdicting, in the sense that it prohibits his perception of the outside and also in the sense that it cuts off his speech, as it does not permit the prolongation of his poem or the play of his imagination. The following poem will make that interdiction clearer:

Petit Poème

Je me souviens de ma chambre d'enfant. La mousseline des rideaux sur la vitre était griffonnée de passementeries blanches, je m'efforçais d'y retrouver l'alphabet et quand je tenais les lettres, je les transformais en dessins que j'imaginais. H, un homme assis; B, l'arche d'un pont sur un fleuve. Il y avait dans la chambre plusieurs coffres et des fleurs ouvertes sculptées légèrement sur le bois. Mais ce que je préférais, c'était deux boules de pilastre qu'on apercevait derrière les rideaux et que je considérais comme des têtes de pantins avec lesquels il était défendu de jouer.

(41; p. 157)

In this poem, Max Jacob's reverie is doubly transposed. He first transforms the curtain's trim into letters of the alphabet, which he then imagines as drawings: "H" takes the form of a man seated; "B," inclined horizontally, resembles a bridge. These different transpositions of perceived phenomena invite the reader to pursue the game: "un homme assis," "l'arche d'un pont sur un fleuve"; it only takes "sur" to complete the image of a man contemplating suicide—a sugges-

2. "Les Fenêtres," *Petits Poèmes en prose (Le spleen de Paris)* (1869; rpt. Paris: Garnier, 1962), p. 173.

tion reinforced by the coffinlike chests with the floral carvings. This initial reverie is generated by certain objects inside the room, but what he desires most is without, barely glimpsed behind the drapes; he is therefore unable to approach it and cannot "take hold" of it ("je tenais") as he did the letters: outside are two pilaster tops, which he transforms into jumping-jack heads.

It is as if the poet sought to transform the transparency revealing the outside into a reflection of the inside, since by transforming the pilaster tops into jumping jacks he indulges in a certain play with the outside (which, in the preceding poem, had been inaccessible); he brings them forward to the interior in order to become part of the reflected tableau. As part of that reflection the balls of pilaster would be able to permit identification which, for Max Jacob, is akin to a sighting in a mirror. But, once initiated, the play halts, the poet imposes his own restrictions, his own obstacles: he forbids himself a second transformation (he will not allow himself to play with the jumping jacks), and thereby arrests the reader's play: without this second transformation (changing the jumping jacks into the unknown factors, "X," "jouer avec les pantins"), he cannot effect the third as he did with the "H" and the "B" on the trim. For the play to continue, one of its viable features must itself be obviated; the fact of play must not become explicit because, once play becomes self-conscious, it ceases to be. The continuation of play and the process of identification must, in other words, be innocent; they must appear to be proceeding by chance:

Poème

Quand le bateau fut arrivé aux îles de l'océan Indien, on s'aperçut qu'on n'avait pas de cartes. Il fallut descendre! Ce fut alors qu'on connut qui était à bord: il y avait cet homme sanguinaire qui donne du tabac à sa femme et le lui reprend. Les îles étaient semées partout. En haut de la falaise, on aperçut de petits nègres avec des chapeaux melon: "Ils auront peut-être des cartes!" Nous prîmes le chemin de la falaise: c'était une échelle de corde; le long de l'échelle, il y avait peut-être des cartes! des cartes même japonaises! nous montions toujours. Enfin, quand il n'y eut plus d'échelons (des cancres en ivoire, quelque part), il fallut monter avec le poignet. Mon frère l'Africain s'en acquitta très bien, quant à moi, je découvris des échelons où il n'y en avait pas. Arrivés en haut, nous sommes sur un mur; mon frère saute. Moi, je suis à la fenêtre! jamais je ne pourrai me décider à sauter: c'est un mur de planches rouges: "Fais le tour", me crie mon frère l'Africain. Il n'y a plus ni étages, ni passagers, ni bateau, ni petit nègre; il y a le tour qu'il faut faire. Quel tour? c'est décourageant.

(*10*; p. 46)

The title of this poem prepares the reader for an entrance into a poetic realm; but crossing the threshold places him in a world so like the one he has just left that he wonders whether a threshold has in fact been crossed. He encounters such banalities as a ship, maps, geographical sights, and even a historical tone. Yet, with this same certainty and linguistic clarity, we pass into a certain mental and geographic disorientation which is indicated by "on s'aperçut qu'on n'avait pas de cartes." Without maps, how is it possible to know that the Indian Ocean—and not some other point—has been reached?

The ship in the poem might be seen as a parody of Rimbaud's "Bateau ivre," several aspects of which it recalls in an exaggerated form. Like Rimbaud's, it is in search of an "I," as indicated by the fact that "un homme sanguinaire" alights from it. In this regard, it is useful to recall the following remarks from the Preface to *Le Cornet à dés*: "Le style, c'est l'homme même; ce qui signifie qu'un écrivain doit écrire avec son sang" (*1*; p. 19). In both cases, there is exaggeration and whimsy. It seems as if Max Jacob is playing the romantic game with new means which undermine it. Here, the boat would be the poet who does not know himself, who is unaware of what he contains. Yet he is beginning to learn the boat's contents—disembarkation begins (as if we were dealing with Noah's ark); a bloodthirsty man and his wife emerge first, followed by . . . but the enumeration ends there, it is destroyed. The man gives his wife some tobacco and reclaims it immediately—still another automatically eradicated construction.

Double Play

The aim of Max Jacob's search in "Poème"—that is, the stakes that the poet stands to win—is not as mysterious as in the preceding poems. We are again dealing with an identification, but one which, this time, is plainly tied to conflict between two modes of writing: the one prosaic (intended here only in its strictest sense: relating to prose), attempting to give a linear account of a voyage, and the other textual: putting forth a minimal effort to weave a textual fabric: "îles semées" are connected to "tobacco" (tobacco is sown) and to "derby hats" ("chapeaux melon"—melons are also sown and the form of the hats is like that of the sown islands). But the analogy goes no further, it is not systematically reinforced throughout the poem in the way in which someone like Francis Ponge might have done; there is only a feigned hint of unity which delicately seeks to assert itself.

From this perspective, the poem becomes simultaneously both a constructor and a destroyer, and the stakes, once gained, are automatically relinquished. Several juxtapositions betray this double nature: in "des cartes, même japonaises" the maps are a means of guiding the poet, they are familiar and could give a certain security, but their being Japanese suggests incomprehension, mystery. The Japanese maps are signs which initiate communication but which destroy it as automatically as the sanguinary man annuls his exchange. The same phenomenon can also be seen in "je découvris des échelons où il n'y en avait pas" and in "(des cancres en ivoire, quelque part)," the latter being the only image in the poem capable of satisfying the poetic criteria of the past century, but the phenomenon is also one which is obscured by the fact that it is only "somewhere" and between parentheses; further, compared to the strong black wrists of the African brother, it is uncertain and ephemeral.

This self-destructive progression must necessarily come to an end, but to do so, it must change form: "Arrivés en haut, nous sommes sur un mur; mon frère saute. Moi, je suis à la fenêtre. Jamais je ne pourrai me décider à sauter." The poet reaches the impassable window, the peak of the hill and apogee of the poem. Three tenses (past, present, and future) occur in rapid succession and precipitate the action of the text which, until that moment, had been in the historical past. The future ("Je ne pourrai") coincides with the impossibility of jumping out the window because, once the future has been reached in this temporal journey, the poet can only start the cycle again from the past. Thus, when the poet encounters the obstacle, the linear voyage becomes circular. In addition, it becomes internalized, as indicated by the fact that the detached and distant journey in the past suddenly becomes alive and immediate with the succession of tenses. The exterior and linear journey once internalized becomes a circle, an agonizing and paralyzing "tour": "'Fais le tour', me crie mon frère l'Africain." Once the poet becomes conscious of this "tour," this anguishing, mysterious circle ("Quel tour?"), all he has experienced up to that point collapses: "Il n'y a plus ni étages, ni passagers, ni bateau, ni petit nègre," and the "tour" alone dominates. The linear journey gives way to a new form in which the impasse reigns: "Il y a le tour qu'il faut faire."

The circle, it would seem, is of the same order as the textual production which I spoke of above, for if the poet is able to rid himself of the self-destructive, linear, and goal-seeking prose, he will successfully enter the world of the nonreferential text. The prose poem actually seeks to attain textuality by overcoming its own prosaic form. "Poème de la lune," although ending on a note of uncertainty, nevertheless does succeed in triumphing over its prose and forming a text. It does not, however, do so by weaving analogies, as Max Jacob attempted in the preceding poem (see the discussion of "semées"), but rather by weaving metamorphoses—a device which already announces a favorite technique of the surrealists:

Poème de la lune

Il y a sur la nuit trois champignons qui sont la lune. Aussi brusquement que chante le coucou d'une horloge, ils se disposent autrement à minuit chaque mois. Il y a dans le jardin

des fleurs rares qui sont de petits hommes couchés, cent, c'est
les reflets d'un miroir. Il y a dans ma chambre obscure une
navette lumineuse qui rôde, puis deux . . . des aérostats phos-
phorescents, c'est les reflets d'un miroir. Il y a dans ma tête
une abeille qui parle.

(14; p. 76)

Making use of both the language of children (mushrooms,
cuckoo, little men, phosphorescent airships) and a language
of a rigorous certainty (repetitions of "there are" [il y a] and
of the verb "to be") which is constantly destroyed, this poem
traces the stages of a progression toward the interior.

In the first sentence, Max Jacob establishes a rigid identity
between a trinity and a unity. But the latter is summarily destroyed by a kind of mechanical magic, because, as soon as
the mushrooms "se disposent autrement," the moon is replaced by little prone men, "a hundred" of them, a kind of
multiplied, blurred unity. This blur is what indicates that the
poet is facing a window which, because it is nighttime, reflects
the interior of the room; in fact he states that "c'est les reflets
d'un miroir." If the poet is inside the room, his view is partially impaired by the reflections from within, the window
doubling as a mirror which reflects a blurred, unstable "I."
But shortly, with difficulty, the outside penetrates the room.
The exactly parallel constructions of the four sentences beginning with "il y a" suggest that a metamorphosis of the elements has occurred from one sentence to the next. The metamorphoses move toward the poet, coming closer and closer
to him. First the setting which the poet envisions moves toward him: from "night" it moves to the "garden," then to the
"room," and finally becomes completely internalized when it
passes into his "head." The object sought after (the moon)
also undergoes a series of metamorphoses as it changes contexts: the "mushrooms" become "flowers," then an "incense
holder," and finally, when it becomes internalized, an incoher-
ent bee. Simultaneously with the evolution of the elements,
the unity in the first sentence becomes a blurred hundred
and is then flatly destroyed by "une navette . . . qui rôde, puis
deux. . . ." When the poet finally internalizes the observed

phenomenon, there is a return to unity with *a* bee, but this unity is one which communicates nothing, it simply buzzes. The moon was therefore able to pass through the window and the poet did succeed, with difficulty, in apprehending it: it had to pass through a series of metamorphoses, mirrors, and destructions to end up as a talking bee. The metamorphoses and destructions facilitated the passage, but they also reduced the moon to a bee whose buzzing cannot communicate the moon. "Poème de la lune" is nevertheless the result of weaving the stages of experience. From this point of view, Max Jacob succeeded in constructing his text and in taking the "tour" presented in the preceding poem.

Transparency and Opacity

I would like at this point to introduce an ambiguity into the roles played by transparency and opacity, interior and exterior.

In "Mystère du ciel" the transparency of the pane functions as an obstacle to the imaginative process which requires "closure" to unfurl and play its game. In "Poème de la lune" the situation is reversed: the opacity of the pane (mirror) plays its true role: it is a physical obstacle to a perception of the exterior. This reversal is not inexplicable: everything depends upon the attitude or the position of the poet at the outset. In "Mystère du ciel" and "Petit poème" his attitude is active (in athletic terms we might say he takes the offensive), whereas in "Poème de la lune" he is passive: the poet is nearly immobile, letting events occur and objects come to him. In accordance with the rules of the latter, the exterior must come to him, and any opacity would function as an obstacle; whereas, in the others, he must go toward the exterior, and the most efficacious means of doing so is to construct it, to fabricate it or imagine it, in which case transparency is harmful and opacity desirable. To go even further, the choice to be made between the passive and active stances may itself constitute an obstacle.

It is therefore possible to say that, in a sense, Max Jacob's search does not distinguish between exterior and interior, that these two do not play the differentiating role which they played in Baudelaire's poetry, where the exterior was always to be internalized; instead, for Max Jacob, the transgression from one to the other, the projection of the one into the other is what defines their role in his search. In the case of "Vie double," there is no need for the obstacle to become manifest; it is constructed initially by the hesitation between two poles: passivity and activity.

> Vie double
> Le château a deux tours pointues et nous nous allongeons sur le mamelon d'en face. La vieille demoiselle a l'air d'un maître-autel; le perron du château a l'air d'un maître-autel et le voilà qui s'envole vers nous soutenu par des colombes. Or, ce maître-autel laissait tomber des prospectus: *Vente de charité*. Et la demoiselle m'en offrit un sans s'apercevoir que j'avais plus de droit à être le vendu que le vendant, l'acheté que l'acheteur et le bénéficiaire que le bénéficiant.
>
> (*21*; p. 85)

The hillock, the two towers, and doubtless the sky above recall a game of hopscotch in which the poet, waiting for the sky to come to him, plays a passive role. Moreover, it is not surprising to find a "maître-autel," high altar, in the poem because the game of hopscotch, as well as the castle in the poem, are in the shape of a cross. In the second sentence, the setting is transformed into the scene of a potential erotic exchange. Comparing the spinster to the high altar has the effect of suggesting the enormity of her breasts (mamelon); the steps are then also compared to the high altar and thus become equally large.

This religio-erotic triptych will be, in a manner of speaking, internalized by the poet, as it is God's message which is delivered from the altar and because the altar "laissait tomber des prospectus." The message is nevertheless not free of charge, since this is a *Vente de charité* which calls for the poet's giving something in exchange. At the moment when the poet realizes that the message is part of an exchange, the triptych is retransformed into an aged spinster who has lost all her imaginary value, and the poem which, up to that point, had been oneiric or poetic, suddenly also becomes prosaic. The loss of poetry is due to a sudden self-consciousness; the poet becomes aware of what had been suggested in the first part of the poem, that he is playing a passive role, and this realization functions as an obstacle which inhibits him. This awareness puts a stop to all communication between the sky and the poet because the latter realizes that he has nothing to offer in exchange and that, instead of being the buyer, the seller, or the benefactor, the author of the exchange, he is its passive object: the sold, the bought, the beneficiary. His life is therefore double because he can act as if he were playing an active role while he is unaware of his passive nature, or be passive once he has understood that nature.

The poet's lack of awareness is his only means of eliminating the ambiguity and it is also a prerequisite for play; in order for there to be play, in order for the game to be salvaged, it must not be recognized as play. Once the player becomes aware of his nature (passive/active), the game is destroyed and the "poetic" becomes "prosaic." There is a reversal in the text; what was active becomes passive, symbolized in this text by the castle's two pointed towers, which the poet contemplates as if he were hesitating between the two—"as if" because the transformation has already occurred, since he has already opted (naturally without knowing it) for the passive tower.

Switches

Until now, passivity and activity have been stated in only the most diffuse terms, vaguely linked to an initial position and its reversal and, more importantly, to the mode of writing (poetic/prosaic). This dichotomy can be delineated more clearly in another text, similar to the one we have just read, where the active/passive roles take the form author/character, manipulator/manipulated. The obstacle has not disappeared; it again takes the form of a hesitation which, in this case, is depicted as a geometrical point situated at infinity:

Nocturne des hésitations familiales

Il y a des nuits qui finissent dans une gare! Il y a des gares
qui finissent dans les nuits. En avons-nous traversé des rails la
nuit! moi, je me suis fait rudoyer par des angles extérieurs de
wagon la nuit: j'en ai encore mal au deltoïde. Quand on atten-
dait la sœur aînée, ou le père, cela finissait par ce qu'on
n'avoue pas: la paire de souliers arrosée de la farine du pain.
Mais j'ai un frère qui est désagréable dans une gare: il n'arrive
qu'au dernier moment (il a des principes), alors il faut rouvrir
une valise qu'un domestique n'avait pas encore apportée;
même devant le guichet, il ne sait pas encore sur quelle gare il
doit faire diriger les wagons: il hésite entre Nogent-sur-Marne
et les Ponts-de-Cé ou autres. La valise est là, ouverte! Son billet
n'est pas acquis et les becs de gaz essaient en vain de transformer la nuit en jour ou le jour en nuit. Il y a des nuits qui
finissent dans une gare, des gares qui finissent dans la nuit.
Ah! maudite hésitation, n'est-ce pas toi qui m'as perdu, et bien
ailleurs que dans vos salles d'attente, ô gares!

(27; p. 97)

The poet cannot decide between "des nuits qui finissent
dans une gare" and "des gares qui finissent dans les nuit"—
that is, again, between two different modes of writing. The
first is prosaic in that it has a duration in time and suggests
an anecdote in which a character spends the night in a station, no doubt awaiting someone's arrival. The second is pictorial in that, instead of a character and a narrative, it deals
with an author who apprehends and composes a perspective
drawing depicting a station fading into the night. If the spectator viewing the canvas were to neglect the fact that it is a
linear perspective, he would see an angle whose summit is in
the center of the upper portion of the frame. Considered simultaneously, the two sentences with their opposing meanings each present angles, one present, the other hypothetical,
whose summits touch. Yet it is notably the first sentence, the
anecdotal sentence, the one which might be qualified as
"real," which constitutes the hypothetical angle because it is
not drawn; only the second, the one that forms the perspective, is visible.

The entire poem is thus constructed on this double angularity whose center is the arrival point of one angle-sentence and the point of departure of the other: the station where one arrives and from which one leaves, in which the poet hesitates between one angle and another, between character and author, between narration which takes place in time and painting which is apprehended instantly. The poem appears to relate a story: rails are crossed, people jostle one another, they wait for the father, the older sister, or the brother who arrives at the last minute and who loses his ticket. . . . But these very anecdotal sentences betray pictorial elements. In "En avons-nous traversé des rails la nuit" it is already possible to detect an angular structure in the penumbra in which parallel tracks connect at infinity; these same angles are evoked by "des angles extérieurs," which become internal with "deltoïde," a triangular muscle. The rough treatment is thus as much physical as mental, the hesitation is both superficial (where to go?) and profound. In this context the sentence "cela finissait par ce qu'on n'avoue pas" is tautological: we end up at the peak of the angle, at infinity, at what is not acknowledged, "par ce qu'on *n'avoue* pas," etymologically at what cannot be made one's own: an insignificant remark like "la paire de souliers arrosée de la farine du pain." The sentence "il n'arrive qu'au dernier moment" is another tautology because in this context one can only arrive at the last minute, at the end, where the parallels meet—which is why the brother "has principles" (geometrical or other!).

The brother, like the poet, is irresolute, not only because "il ne sait pas encore sur quelle gare il doit faire diriger les wagons," but also because, like the poet, he is alternately character and author, passenger and conductor. We see him arrive, open his bag, and suddenly he has vast powers: he directs traffic. This hesitation is again stressed in the image of the suitcase which, when open, forms an angle which invites closing. Finally, in "les becs de gaz essaient en vain de transformer la nuit en jour ou le jour en nuit" we again find the agonizing double angularity: the light rays which emanate from the gas lamps form angles whose summit is the source of light, but these rays can travel in both directions: they may change "night into day *or* day into night." The poem ends as it began, in the anguish of hesitation: the first two sentences are repeated in a kind of refrain reminiscent of a musical nocturne, and the disorientation is solemnly declared with "n'est-ce pas toi qui m'as perdu." "Perdu" thus acquires several meanings: the poet is lost in the station, he loses the sense of his poetic orientation, that is, his ability to decide between playing the author or the character, and, finally, he is lost in the sense of ruined, declaring thereby the failure of the poem.

Playing to Lose

Even if there is unawareness and hence play, and even if the poet overcomes the obstacle which separates him from the object (or the reverie), Max Jacob arranges things so that the victory is negated, so that playing involves losing:

Frontispice

Oui, il est tombé du bouton de mon sein et je ne m'en suis pas aperçu. Comme un bateau sort de l'ancre du rocher avec les marins sans que la mer en frémisse davantage, sans que la terre sente cette aventure nouvelle, il est tombé de mon sein de Cybèle un poème nouveau et je ne m'en suis pas aperçu.

(*13*; p. 75)

Since a breast is shaped like a dice cup, it can be said that the poem which falls from it is a new configuration of the dice capable of revealing something to the poet. But once again the poet is playing a passive role which negates revelation, for, if the sea had quivered as it did for Rimbaud's "Bateau ivre," if the earth had sensed the adventure, the poet would have been aware of his production at the moment at which it occurred. Yet it slipped away forever into the void without leaving a trace, without the poet's taking notice. The result is thus only a frontispiece, an exterior which impedes inward-directed reverie. It could therefore be stated that even if Max Jacob managed to play the game, to throw the dice successfully, the result would invariably be negative because they were not intentionally thrown; instead, they fall by chance, and are thus unable to reveal anything to him concerning his search.

Up to this point (with the exception of "Frontispiece"), unawareness was a prerequisite for playing and losing or, more precisely, non-play was associated with awareness. Yet in this poem both play and unawareness coexist. There is also loss, and it is precisely because it was not noticed (unawareness) that loss occurred. Once again the dichotomy is reduced. The two poles and their meanings are not, in themselves, significant; it is their breakdown which has significance. It should be noted that if there is a constant to be found in Max Jacob's writing it does not lie in an opposition between specific series (exterior/interior, passive/active, awareness/unawareness), but rather in a structure of their systematic reduction, in the manner in which they break one another down. Initially exterior and interior (and, by extension, transparency and opacity) were set as opposites, but soon they switched places and the obstacle still remained. It was then discovered that the terms of the passive/active opposition (which also reflected the opposition between poetic and prosaic) were also interchangeable, having been superseded by the obstacle of a choice to be made between them; and, finally, the cardinal rule of the game, unawareness, did give way to awareness, but loss *nevertheless* occurred. It seems as though there is always a beyond, always a new obstacle which is of necessity invented, generated by each setback. Something new will always come from *Le Cornet à dés*; the form of the text is theoretically limited because the total number of configurations could be eventually reached, but the meanings which can be assigned to them, the games to be played, are limitless: at each throw of the dice, a way must be found either not to count them (no play) or to lose, and it is precisely this loss which is vital, indispensable to continued play, to beginning again and writing a new poem. In other words, without loss (obstacle) there can be no play, and it is because there is loss that play persists.

4 ⬡

Masks

Mais de la tête jusqu'au cœur
Le poète est un imposteur
—Max Jacob, *Les Pénitents en maillots roses*

Reading Max Jacob led to the discovery in the last chapter that at the base of the generation of his poems lay a tendency to reduce dichotomies systematically, to break down contraries and contradictions. Taking a slightly larger perspective of the poems, however, reveals a contradiction which has, until now, remained irreducible: on the one hand Max Jacob seems to say that he is unable to effect an exchange, to transgress or to play (win), while, on the other hand, he does successfully construct and present poems which, if they are not play, at least communicate its impossibility. In other words, the dice are imprisoned in the dice cup, yet they are simultaneously thrown.

> ## Le Bibliophile
> La reliure du livre est un grillage doré qui retient prisonniers des cacatoès aux mille couleurs, des bateaux dont les voiles sont des timbres-poste, des sultanes qui ont des paradis sur la tête pour montrer qu'elles sont très riches. Le livre retient prisonnières des héroïnes qui sont très pauvres, des bateaux à vapeur qui sont très noirs et de pauvres moineaux gris. L'auteur est une tête prisonnière d'un grand mur blanc (je fais allusion au plastron de sa chemise).
>
> *(44*; p. 186)

The book in this poem imprisons its content and at the same time discloses it, as does Max Jacob's dice cup and this collection of poems, *Le Cornet à dés*. The content cannot go beyond the binding and reach the bibliophile (reader) because the binding forms a gilt lattice which prevents anything from emerging. This reader is in a situation analogous to that of the poet who tries to discover the "Mystère du ciel," who sought to "read" certain signs which would permit an identification. Both are unable to open the book (whether it be real or metaphorical) and thereby permit the content to reach them; both fail, in short, to play the game or throw the dice. For the actual readers—ourselves—of this poem, however, there is a transgression, albeit a contradictory one. "Cacatoès" are birds of the parrot family, but they are also the sails of a schooner. These sails reoccur in the next element: "des bateaux dont les voiles sont des timbres-postes." They represent transportation and hence mark a liberation from the binding, but they are also veils, obstacles, of the type worn by the sultanas mentioned in the third item of the enumeration. They serve thus a dual function: one of imaginary transportation and another of physical restriction. In fact, the sultanas simultaneously evoke both of these qualities: they wear veils and "ont des paradis sur la tête," which is to say that they dream of flight, if "paradis" is taken for birds of paradise, or of heaven and desire to be free of their enslavement. The second itemization of the contents of this book is the exact opposite of the first. Instead of wealthy sultanas there are poor heroines, instead of sailboats, black steamboats, and instead of multicolored cockatoos, or birds of paradise, "poor grey sparrows." The interesting fact here is that the same book contains both antithetical categories, things both rich and poor at the same time, black and white at the same time. Almost the same duality composes *Le Cornet à dés*: the dice are cast and they are not; the poet both is and is not a prisoner; he is unable to communicate yet does. It is interesting that the author of the book in question is, like the poet of *Le Cornet à dés*, "une tête prisonnière d'un grand mur blanc" and that, like the poet, he is a player, reducing his agonizing prison into a shirtfront, a laughter-provoking whim akin to the device used with the sultanas: their desire to flee the harem is reduced to an overloaded hat: "Elles ont des paradis sur la tête pour montrer qu'elles sont très riches."

A Throw of the Dice

Like the content of "Le Bibliophile," which both does and does not emerge, each of the poems in *Le Cornet à dés* is a potential configuration of a throw of the dice. In this putative game of dice, the poet, unable to play against anyone, plays against chance, which is to say, against himself. His fate is in play with each throw of the dice because he alone throws them. Each presumed configuration of the dice is a reflection of this fate as it might be written in himself and in the cosmos (the face of the dice resembling a starry sky). Thus, ideally, each poem could become a mirror of the poet's astrological and physiological identity. Self-revelation is ultimately the aim of the game:

> Succès de la confession
> Sur la route qui mène au champ de course, il y avait un mendiant pareil à un domestique: "Ayez pitié, disait-il, je suis vicieux, j'irai jouer avec l'argent que vous me donnerez." Et ainsi de suite sa confession. Il avait un grand succès et il le méritait.
>
> (*24*; p. 90)

This poem acquires an air of morality as a result of the underlying simple causal statement: "sincerity pays." Yet it is necessary to look beyond the aphorism in order to understand the poem, because it is especially from the destruction of this causality—which is again transformed into circularity—that the poem derives its value. The apparent causality is as follows: the beggar confesses in order to obtain money, he bets with the money, loses it, and then returns to beg for more. But, since this man is "vicieux," since his nature is, in a manner of speaking, circular (just like the racetrack), nothing prevents our starting at any step in the process. We might say that he is given money to gamble, that he gambles in order to confess, and so on, viciously. Separating one of the steps in the cycle, we arrive at "he plays in order to confess" and thus in order to know himself, for it is only when he confesses that he reveals himself as vicious. This is a revelation for both the passerby and the beggar, as well as for the structure of the poem. The beggar thus plays to disclose his identity, in the same manner as the Poet of *Le Cornet à dés*. Both play a game of chance and, as I shall suggest, both must attempt some form of exchange in order to carry out their play.

The Mask

It might again be stressed that this is only a potential game, one which might have occurred had there been no obstacles, but which, in fact, is not actualized. The game must nevertheless exist, because we have the evidence of the poems before us. We too must, therefore, join in the game and consent to accept a fiction: we must presume that the poems are written, the dice cast, and the "I" revealed. In order for the fiction (which isn't one, since the poems are actually written) to be sustained, a ground common to the poet and the reader must be found.[1] The mask constitutes this common ground: since the dice are confined in the dice cup, the poet must act *as if* he were throwing them in order to discover his astrological and physiological identities, he acts *as if* he had overcome the obstacle. He wears the mask of success, but this mask must not be viewed in a negative light; the mask is not designed to conceal anything; on the contrary, the mask is an aid to self-discovery, as is suggested by the case of Max Jacob's Tartufe, who must pass through bigotry to become devout.[2] The poet is totally aware of his mask and hence constantly reminds the reader that he has appropriated a role which he would like to call his own but which does not belong to him. The awareness

1. That ground could possibly be called a "playground," according to D. W. Winnicott, for whom it is a "potential space." See his *Playing and Reality* (London: Tavistock, 1971; rpt. London: Penguin Books, 1974), p. 55.
2. See his *Défense de Tartufe* (1919; rpt. Paris: Gallimard, 1964).

of the mask is evident throughout the collection: pastiches and parodies are repeatedly acknowledged by the poet for what they are. Among instances of this tendency are titles which appropriate modes foreign to them, such as "Genre biographique," "Poème dans un goût qui n'est pas le mien," "Poème déclamatoire," "Dans une manière qui n'est pas la mienne," or which suggest fables: "La tante, la tarte et le chapeau," "Le Coq et la perle," "Fable sans moralité," etc. Each poem, each potential throw of the dice, once fixed on the page, thus takes the form of a third mirror reflecting the true image (in the optical sense of the term) of the poet as player: masked, he throws the dice to escape temporarily the lot of a player unable to play, and gives himself a semblance of strength which both he and the reader nevertheless recognize as false. He wears different masks in order to embody this strength, in order to win the game, because it is only by playing (or in this case simulating play) that he can hope to win and become what he pretends to be.

It is now clear that Max Jacob's play is not a dialectic between being and seeming, but rather an effort, a tension, between them. Max Jacob's poetry is the result of this futile effort, an effort destined to inevitable failure because this mask, like that of the good clown or even of his own Tartufe, betrays the predicament of the poet trapped by his inability to communicate. In fact, his poetry has often been characterized as burlesque because of its farcical and comical aspects, because, in other words, of its playfulness. Yet it also warrants that epithet because, like the good burlesque actor, it announces the fact that it plays and thereby reveals the underlying dilemma. When Sartre says that the poet is not involved in the affairs of men,[3] (by which he means that the poet is endowed with superhuman powers and his use of language prevents him from interacting with other men), he may be accurately describing the romantic poets, but such a characterization is inapplicable to Max Jacob, for whom the poet is very much a man, even a weak man, an ineffectual writer weaving not so much texts as rags, false texts, masks.

3. *Qu'est ce que la littérature?* (1948; rpt. Paris: Gallimard, 1967), p. 19.

Rags, Texts

La Rue Ravignan

"On ne se baigne pas deux fois dans le même fleuve", disait
le philosophe Héraclite. Pourtant, ce sont toujours les mêmes
qui remontent! Aux mêmes heures, ils passent gais ou tristes.
Vous tous, passants de la rue Ravignan, je vous ai donné les
noms des défunts de l'Histoire! Voici Agamemnon! voici Mme
Hanska! Ulysse est un laitier! Patrocle est au bas de la rue
qu'un Pharaon est près de moi. Castor et Pollux sont les dames
du cinquième. Mais toi, vieux chiffonnier, toi, qui, au féerique
matin, viens enlever les débris encore vivants quand j'éteins
ma bonne grosse lampe, toi que je ne connais pas, mystérieux
et pauvre chiffonnier, toi, chiffonnier, je t'ai nommé d'un nom
célèbre et noble, je t'ai nommé Dostoïevsky.

(*17*; p. 79)

As is the case in many other poems, the poet stands behind
a window, but here it is transparent and does not function as
an obstacle. From his window he watches a procession of pedestrians whom he has often seen pass by at these same
hours. Because the window is transparent, this procession
can be transformed and taken for a circus parade (like
clowns, the pedestrians who pass are "gais ou tristes"). The
poet bestows masks upon them, he gives them the names
(nothing but the names—which is to say that he ascribes them
identities without changing them internally) of legendary
characters: Agamemnon, Ulysses, Patroclus. . . . He gives
them those names which permit their momentarily escaping
time and their earthly condition. When he gets to the ragpicker, the man who collects yesterday's refuse, including the
scraps of the poet's own nightly work, he calls him Dostoyevsky. The ragpicker thus also becomes a poet, in fact the poet
himself, transported along with the paltry scraps of a night
spent shredding or weaving texts ("quand j'éteins ma bonne
grosse lampe"). The transportation through the window is
achieved by the poet's borrowing the ragpicker's mask and by
lending the ragpicker his own: they become one, having both
escaped their fate by becoming the immortal Dostoyevsky. It
should be noted that the poet becomes Dostoyevsky-rag-

picker in order to know him and to know himself, for he says of the other, "toi que je ne connais pas, mystérieux et pauvre chiffonnier." It is therefore only by wearing the mask of another and by revealing his own mask that the poet can escape his fate and know himself.

It is interesting to note that Baudelaire also likened the poet to a ragpicker in a poem entitled "Le Vin des chiffonniers." A comparison will permit us to examine their radically dissimilar conceptions of the poet. For Baudelaire, it appears that the ragpicker can acquire extraordinary poetic powers through the help of a catalyst: wine. Drunk, he transforms Paris and the inhabitants of a squalid neighborhood into a glorious scene of fermenting wine and carnage. The difference between his and Max Jacob's conception of the poet is remarkable:

> Il prête des serments, dicte des lois sublimes,
> Terrasse les méchants, relève les victimes. . . .[4]

As a poet, he effortlessly becomes a superman, an evangelist, even a savior. For Max Jacob, on the other hand, the transition from ragpicker and man-poet to poet is an extremely difficult one, one brought about not through change, as with Baudelaire's drunkenness, but by an external one: they borrow a famous name (Dostoyevsky), a superficial mask with which they hope to identify and thereby escape their temporality.

The Absence of Meaning: Language

Throughout my discussion of these texts, I have referred to an a priori category which I designated alternately as "earthly condition," "fate of man," etc. It is necessary at this point to note the fictitiousness of this category, because it is established or defined nowhere in Max Jacob's texts; on the

---

4. "He takes oaths, dictates sublime laws, / Floors the wicked, raises the victims," *Les Fleurs du mal* (1857; rpt. Paris: Éditions Garnier, 1961), pp. 120–21. My translation.

contrary, the only evidence of the category is in the effort to be free of it, an effort which presupposes the category but which also undermines it. This category is therefore a fiction, made up by the reader, and the poet as well: the "human," "earthly," or "temporal" condition is no less a fiction than the fabricated image of the "self," the "self-knowledge," toward which the poet aspires. Once again, the nearly continuous generation of texts finds its justification: the poet tries to escape a "human condition" which is vague, undefined, virtually nonexistent, in order to reach an equally amorphous and fictitious "self," based only on masks, texts, and fiction, that lies beyond it.

The mask is ultimately the goal and the means of the quest. There is only firmly established play, play which strives to reach the self but which never gets beyond itself, play which constitutes the only possible "knowledge" and which can lead only to the generation of yet another text. In other words, this "knowledge" is lateral, as opposed to profound: the mask is a signifier without a signified or, more precisely, with a signified which may assume two forms and thereby preclude "meaning" ("meaning" here has the form of self-knowledge or the human condition): the one leads to the generation of further texts, the other to signification, to the rediscovery of the mask-poem as a series of texts within texts. For if there were a meaning, if there were a true "I," it would have long since been found, unmasked and recovered, once and for all; in such a case, the play would be closed and would end with the winning of the game. But here the game is never won, which is precisely why there is a recycling (a victory of sorts), a continuous recasting which repeats an endlessly varied text.

This argument leads us to Max Jacob's definition of art: "L'art est la volonté de s'extérioriser par des moyens choisis" (*1*; p. 21), an apparently banal and classic definition, yet one which, literally, marks a complete breakdown of the romantic esthetic (even though stated in terms taken from that esthetic). Apart from the equivalence of the "means," which the surrealists adamantly proclaimed, apart from the fact that art is a "will" and does not need to be given form, what emerges from this context is the quasi-complete subversion of the sub-ject, the "s apostrophe" of "*s'extérioriser*" is totally fictitious, it is unknown a priori; the mask-poems strive in vain to locate it. Only the "chosen means" remain, the artifices, which are nothing but the poems themselves. In this sense, the mask is the means of projecting onto an imaginary scene with the in-tent of constituting the poetic persona (the "*s'*"), but with no assurance of success.

On the contrary, this projection is assured of failure be-cause of a quality inherent to the persona: he is false and stands to be exposed as such. Once exposed, there is *nothing* behind him, only a lack longing to be satisfied. And the game must begin again. In other words, for Max Jacob the poet starts out with a belief in the existence of and a desire to lo-cate a constituted and constituting self (the idealistic self of the romantics). Initially, the surpassing of the obstacle is thought to lead to discovery of the self, but this surpassing (writing, the poem itself) is an invention, a false "I" appro-priated to effect the identification, an artificial subject, an il-lusion, a game. This amounts to saying that the transgression takes place in an imaginary realm, that of art, artifice proper. In this sense, Max Jacob's writing serves as a pivot between two esthetics. On the one hand it posits a belief in an idealistic self, and on the other it marks the impossibility of attaining it. And it is this very belief in an identity that can never be established which constitutes the necessary and vital obstacle which again promotes rewriting and repetition, and gener-ates not a single being but a multiplicity.

Further, the mask-poem plays (no doubt consciously) the role of representing this same, in some ways latent, conflict. In the preceding pages we have examined numerous poems which introduced two opposing forces, whether in terms of writing (text/prose), of attitude (passive/active), or even of barriers (transparency/opacity). Writing is thus the means of resolving the conflict; what is originally latent has been made manifest in nearly every poem considered. It is perhaps in this sense that we may speak of a "difference" in poetry, and not in the sense according to which there is a difference between poetry and so-called "everyday" language. Poetry, rather, creates a difference, a distance between itself and a void to keep the void at bay; it momentarily defers a repressed conflict by giving it a form.

This distance is analogous to the "situation" which Max Jacob attributes to art as its second vital principle. As mask, the poem constitutes a mystery and institutes a distance between itself, the poet, and the reader. The reader's play consists of *grasping* the poem, in the intellectual and spatial sense of the term. The reader must, in a sense, demystify the mask, awaken the poet from his reverie, bridge the difference, and reintroduce him into the realm of his lack: the end point, the space after each small poem, the void which gives rise to another text, another difference. Although involved with demystification and unmasking, the reader's activity is evidently not a negative one; he is not a detective intent upon exposing a culprit. On the contrary, he participates in a form of the play whose terms are set forth by the poet in his first lines. The latter admits that he is masked, and invites the reader to unmask him, to "resituate" him, to bring him back to the void, and thus to permit his starting anew. Nor is the demystification of the mask-poem its negation; the reader is not looking behind the "poetic language" for some meaning which might correspond to "what the poet really meant to say"; the reader engages in no form of reduction. Instead, this demystification is the rediscovery of the poem's texture *as surface*, of its existence as a mask which, reconstructed (rewritten), permits the passage (its comprehension and apprehension), the same kind of passage which the poet sought to achieve beyond external phenomena, beyond the obstacles, and which the reader pursues on a parallel axis: that of reading-writing.

There are thus two ways (which are not mutually exclusive) of viewing Max Jacob's poetics, two ways that characterize the ambiguity and instability of which I wrote in my opening chapters. According to one the poet, in search of the self, encounters an obstacle in his path which forces him to invent masks, while the reader follows a similar course in the opposite direction: demystifying the mask. According to the other, the quest itself is an obstacle whose supersession (unconscious, imaginary, and false) lies in writing. The first formulation is prosaic (it traces a path), the second is static or structural, two modes of apprehension which again translate the pivotal status of Max Jacob's writing.

Whatever the formulation (prosaic/structural or linear/profound), the language is the same; it is always expressed in terms of obstacles and masks. In any event, there can be no choice between them. The two modes coexist simultaneously; they intersect. The remaining task is to construct a typology of the points at which they intersect, the sole constants: the poem-mask-obstacles.

5 ⬡

Riddles:
Reading (of) the Surface

In nonsense all the world is
paper and all the seas are ink.
—Elizabeth Sewell, *The Field of Nonsense*

A Four-Handed Hand

According to Johan Huizinga, poetry and play have points in common. The guesser of a riddle, for example, and the reader perform similar activities; the poem and the riddle have similar properties. Poetic language, like the riddle, "is living and noble play" which "disposes images in style, . . . instills mystery into them so that every image contains an answer to an enigma."[1] In other words, for Huizinga poetic language is nothing but an embellishing euphemism or a capricious hermetism concealing a true meaning. The reader would presumably uncover this meaning by dispelling the image. Such a deciphering operation, however, would take into account neither the complexity of Max Jacob's poetry nor the surface texture of his masks. If a comparison were to be made between a poem and a riddle, I would prefer to say that, whereas certain poems in *Le Cornet à dés* do present themselves, fictionally, *as if* they were riddles, they cannot be read as such; that is, they do not have a *hidden* meaning. On the contrary, these texts focus the reader's attention on the

---

1. *Homo Ludens: A Study of the Play Element in Culture* (1938, Eng. trans., Boston: Beacon Press, 1955), p. 134.

48

surface. The poet uses them as masks behind which, once again, nothing is hidden. The reader accepts the mask in a way: he plays the game, pretends to be dealing with a riddle, and treats the text accordingly, in the same way that the poet simulates a riddler. This fiction is not only vital but contagious. Necessarily "contagious" because what was designated up to this point as "reader," "audience" (one may even add the "literary critic") is not as clearly defined and delineated an entity as one might expect. For the poet also functions as a reader and, as reader of his own text, plays a role quite different from that of the writing poet intent upon creating and identifying with a spurious version of "himself" in the text. Unlike the writing poet, who attempts a projection into a fictional scene, the reading poet occupies the same place as the actual reader; he neither identifies with any of the characters nor does he participate vicariously in the activity depicted in the text. Instead, the reading poet remains facing the spurious poetic subject, the idealized and virtual subject, who is fully constituted only in appearance; and the poet undertakes the demystification of that subject.

Were it not for this demystification, a successful identification would be reached through an elimination of the distance between the poetic subject (constructed by the writing poet) and the reading poet—an achievement reminiscent of Proust, who projects an image (to be a writer) which, though initially false, becomes true at the end of the book and with which, through the very process of writing the book, he ultimately identifies (he has become a writer). But this is not the case here, there is always a failure at identification; it seems further that a failure is necessary, for if the narrative text is characterized by the continuing pursuit of a self-image which is only attained at the end, the poetic text depends, perhaps, upon the failure of such an undertaking, a failure through which the lack of self-image *repeatedly* affirms itself and thus guarantees the writing of each text.

Within the play of the riddle, this lack is confirmed by the fact that each text begins with the donning of a new mask, the creation of a new "identity." It is then, in the moments between the texts, when the game is null, the riddle unposed, the mask not yet devised—in short, when, at least theoretically, there is neither poetic subject nor "reader"—that the lack of a unified poetic identity is "manifest." Based on non-play, these moments maintain a precarious balance which is immediately destroyed by the first word produced by the text, a gesture which institutes a disequilibrium between the masked poetic subject (the false image devised by the writer) and his audience (the readers and the reading poet). Once the riddle has been posed, the riddler reigns supreme, superior to his audience and to himself, mystifying both himself and his readers. The reader (as well as the reading poet) recognizes a power in the "subject" which he lacks. To him, the riddler is a sage, a prophet, even a superman who knows far more than he does. This superiority is established by the mask itself, by the fact that the riddle (mask) has been posed, because the reader, intent upon deciphering the riddle, loses sight of the "poseur" behind it. To the reader, the text has become a mask with superhuman powers which permits the subject's escape to higher spheres. Now, he is the one, in effect, possessing the lack, the same kind of lack which prompted the writer to create the mask.

It is now clear that the initial balance was only a working hypothesis. In fact, the lack always exists: in the interstices, after the closure of a text and before the beginning of the next, it is the poet's; in the writing, it is the reader's. To move from the writing to the interstice, in other words to read the text through to its closure, the reader must, as stated, demystify the masked text. But it must again be stressed that this demystification is achieved through a recognition of the mask as material. In other words, the reader refers back to, reflects, the very signs which the poetic subject assumes; he reveals the texture of the poem, its production, its fabrication, its artificiality.

Reading (of) the Surface

I cannot insist too much upon this texture, this surface

from which the poem derives. In a letter to Conrad Moricand, with whom he had collaborated in the writing of *Miroir d'astrologie*, Max Jacob uses a vocabulary that will help clarify some of my points: "Dimanche . . . je t'enverrai des dames "LION", je vais y penser toute la semaine: je les ai dans la peau, il faut les faire sortir."[2] The expression "to have something under one's skin" is closely related to writing. As with Antonin Artaud, for whom writing and thought cause "itching," language here is at the surface, in the skin, and it must be brought out. Later, in the same letter, Max Jacob, complaining of his isolation, writes: "Ma mère et ma sœur sont si j'ose dire la vivante image de ce que j'aurais pu être . . . si je n'étais pas un ancien bachelier, un ancien montmartrois, un chrétien etc. Je suis écorché vif avec l'incapacité de rien dire."[3]

Once again speech is in the skin and the inability to speak is tantamount to being skinned alive. To be speechless is to be skinless. The following paragraph, in which he relates one of his dreams, contains an even more startling revelation. There, the expressions "to have something under one's skin" and "to be skinned alive"—which might have been taken as clichés—are caught up in a network of determinations that betray a serious preoccupation in Max Jacob. Here is the text of his dream: "J'ai rêvé d'un bistrot où Picasso riant me jetait à la figure une branche de persil mouillée de sauce. Puis je touchais un masque coloré de cuir que je chiffonnais, que je gondolais."[4]

2. "Sunday . . . I will send you some 'LEO' ladies; I'll be thinking about it all week: I've got them in my skin, they must be brought out" (Max Jacob, *Lettres, 1920–1941*, ed. S. I. Collier [Oxford: Basil Blackwell, 1966], pp. 58–59). My translation.

3. "My mother and my sister are, if I dare say, the living image of what I could have been . . . were I not a former bachelor [of arts], a former *montmartrois*, a Christian, etc. I am skinned alive by my inability to say anything" (ibid.). My translation.

4. "I dreamt of a bistro where Picasso, laughing, tossed a sprig of parsley dipped in sauce in my face. Then I touched a colored leather mask that I crumpled, that I buckled" (ibid.). My translation.

Since Max Jacob will give his own interpretation of the dream, let us simply note that it has to do with a face and a leather mask, associated through the mention of Picasso with art and creation. This is his interpretation: "J'ai beau chercher, je ne trouve pas le sens. La face est création! Picasso aussi: je comprends le cuir gondolé comme une création qui manquerait de naturel."[5]

Without hesitation, he interprets the face, the mask, as creation. Searching for the meaning or the depths of his dream, he performs what amounts to the opposite: the depths are brought to the surface, to the skin. And if he claims to search hard without finding, it is perhaps the very word "search" that begins to lose its meaning: if the word "search" implies an entire metaphysics of truth and of the subject (as in "Who is the subject of my dream?" and its corollary, "What I dream is what I am, my subject"), here what is "searched" is entirely apparent and present on the surface: "the face is creation." Invoking Picasso in this context is also significant. The mask's "lack of naturalness" could well refer to the lack of depth in some of Picasso's portraits, namely the disposition of figures without perspective and the placement of the entire depicted subject at the surface.[6]

Apollinaire provides a good illustration of such a placement at the surface in "Fenêtres"; the first verse reads: "Du rouge au vert tout le jaune se meurt."[7] Although symbolization might permit ascribing certain meanings to these colors, I prefer to consider the movement described. This movement is indicated by "se meurt," a lateral drift from one color to another, with no emergence of meaning, as Mallarmé

5. "No matter how hard I search, I can't find the meaning. The face is creation! Picasso too: I understand the buckled leather as a creation lacking naturalness" (ibid.). My translation.

6. I am obviously disregarding the friendship between the painter and the poet, as well as the psychological relations this dream could unveil.

7. "From red to green all the yellow dies." (*Calligrammes* [1925; rpt. Paris: Gallimard, Collection "Poésie/Gallimard," 1966], pp. 25–26). My translation.

would surely have provided. This lateral movement is itself explicitly practiced several verses later:

> Tours
>
> Les tours ce sont les rues
>
> Puits
>
> Puits ce sont les places
>
> Puits[8]

We have here an obliteration of height and depth; the towers leveled, flattened, become streets, just as the depth of the wells rises; the bottom is placed at the surface, and the wells become squares. Wells and squares are part of the same tableau depicting, without perspective, the map as well as the content of a city: towers and wells that are streets and squares where movement, traffic, occur precisely at the surface. What Apollinaire achieves with his leveling is to apprehend, at a single level, the map and the territory, the signifier (the map of the city) and the signified (towers, wells) of his subject. The reading is done at the surface, from left to right, from top to bottom and not from the word to its meaning, from the utterance to its origin. This type of reading is no doubt encouraged by the homonymy of "puits" (well) and "puis," meaning "and then; next."

In a short text in *Le Cornet à dés* titled "Patte ou pâte," Max Jacob seems to share Apollinaire's preoccupations. But whereas Apollinaire situated the problem at the level of the figuration of the surface, Max Jacob adds a supplementary element

8. Towers

The towers they are streets

Wells

Wells they are squares

Wells
Ibid. My translation.

which grounds the problem around or in a letter, and therefore in a more superficial and perhaps even more fundamental manner. The poem in question also deals with origins and surfaces, but this time with a corporeal surface:

> Patte ou pâte
> Près de la cheminée, contre le mur, celui qui a un chapeau haut de forme en velours rouge et une trace blanche sur la joue me fait comprendre qu'on a vu Sarah Bernhardt se raser la figure. C'est invraisemblable! quelque marin de Belle-Île l'aura surprise pendant que, se croyant dans les solitudes, elle effaçait des rides avec quelque patte ou pâte.
>
> (*31*; p. 107)

The "trace of white on the cheek" of the one "with the red velvet top hat" could be taken as a scar covered over with some "paste." We might even suspect that his wound resulted from a blow ("coup de patte") by Sarah Bernhardt. If so, we might ask who would have caught her shaving, if not the very man telling the story, the Belle-Île sailor masked with a top hat and makeup (the trace on his cheek); and if he fails to identify himself as the voyeur, it is because Sarah Bernhardt took precautions to silence him with a "coup de patte." The effect of this blow is to prevent the telling of what has been seen, or at least, as in the case of the sailor/narrator, to make him disguise himself in order to tell it.[9]

Taxidermy is therefore one of the conditions of the narrative, the arrangement of the skin and perhaps even the changing of the skin (let us recall one of the aphorisms in the Preface to the *Cornet à dés*: ("To surprise is not much," said Max Jacob, "one must *transplant*," *1*; p. 22), but in this case the skin consists of one letter, the "t" missing from "pâte" or added to "patte." In this vein, there is still another revelation to be made. The sailor comes from "Belle-Île," or *belle* (beau-

---

9. In the following poem dissimulation (wearing of a mask) is not the sole precondition of narration; the origin must also be obliterated in order to tell the story: "C'était un costume de Pierrot en percale, à culotte trop courte même pour le genou et que je louai, le disputant à un certain sergent. J'y ai trouvé des lettres! oui! des lettres que je publierai quand la boutique sera détruite ou le sergent mort" (*12h*; pp. 61–62).

tiful)–*Î*(s)*l*(e) [*il* = he], which must be considered as a kind of androgyny in which the feminine adjective "belle" is the attribute of the masculine pronoun "il." If we recall that Sarah Bernhardt often played masculine roles, the sailor/man in the top hat would be none other than Sarah Bernhardt herself disguised for the occasion. She wears a double mask to tell a story about skin, masks, makeup, and verisimilitude.

Miniatures

I shall continue my discussion of the poem-masks with a minitext—one of the short poems which make up the series "Le Coq et la perle"—which has received considerable critical attention, a rare phenomenon in the literature on Max Jacob:

> L'enfant, l'éfant, l'éléphant, la grenouille et la pomme sautée.
> *(12f*; p. 59)

Dividing the poem into two parts, Yvon Belaval[10] shows that the segment "L'enfant, l'éfant, l'éléphant" forms a rhythmic whole which, although devoid of meaning, reminds the reader of such grammar rhymes learned during childhood as "bijou, caillou, chou. . . ." The unity of the second part is not based on sonority but instead on the dynamics of the image: frogs hop ("saute") just as the cook fries ("fait sauter") the potatoes. Belaval suggests further that the apple ("pomme") could also be one just knocked from a tree ("la fait sauter dans les mains"). This image makes him think of "pommes reinettes" and "rainette," the latter being a type of frog which children often play with. The unity of the poem is thus established for Belaval by a feature common to both parts: the evocation of children's play. This unity is reinforced by the fact that "pomme sautée" could also be read as an apple which was passed over, which was not eaten, hence one which, in biblical terms, evokes a state of innocence. Pursuing Belaval's suggestions, one might say that this is a child who has not yet mastered language, yet who tries to pronounce a difficult word like "éléphant" by using other, simpler terms

10. *La Rencontre avec Max Jacob* (Paris: Charlot, 1947), pp. 39–43.

(either real or invented) such as "enfant" and "éfant." But this does not provide a satisfactory understanding of the poem; these remarks tend instead to read into the text in order to arrive at what lies behind it ("an atmosphere of childlike innocence"). In other words, Belaval treats the text as little more than a vehicle for creating the atmosphere which emerged at first reading and, in that sense, partially ignores the text itself. To demystify the text, it must be de-scribed, "de-texturized," broken down into its components or, in the terms which I have been using, *unmasked* (decompose the mask), or else *read* (attain closure).

The exotic "éfant"[11] is vital to this demystification; placed between "enfant" and "éléphant," it functions as an intermediary term in the progression towards the last word of the text: "sautée." "Enfant," composed of two identical nasal sounds, suggests flatness; the disappearance of one of these nasal sounds and its replacement by an acute "é" in the next word, "éfant," suggests that the sound has risen slightly, in other words that a tiny phonic leap has occurred. The presence of two "é's" in the third element of the enumeration, "éléphant," indicates that the leap has been doubled. Further, "élé," added to the constant ("fant"), recalls the word "élévation." The second part of the poem changes codes by substituting images for sounds: the next term, "grenouille," designates an animal especially noted for its jumping, and the final term, "pomme sautée"—whose "é" reaffirms the correlations between form and content—contains the word "sautée" (in the sense of "leapt") which had been implicit throughout. Although marking the culmination of a progression, the final syllable nevertheless indicates the beginning of a reversal: the tense of "sautée" designates a completed action, and the mute "e" at the end has completely lost the acuteness associated with elevation.

The reader must evidently play an active role when at-

11. The word "éfant" doesn't exist in French. Belaval claims, however, that it means "child" in Breton (Max Jacob was from Brittany).

tempting to reach an understanding of the poem. In fact, the entire poem could be considered as the title—nothing but the title—of a fable. Starting from this title, the reader produces the fable (in the sense of making up a story, in this case a tale of linguistic metamorphoses) in order to demystify the poem, to appropriate it and thereby return the lack to the poet.

A semantic plurality organizes the next short text:

Un diadème est changé en mille têtes de députés.

(*12n*; p. 71)

This constitutes a kind of enchanted metamorphosis whose logic is nevertheless discernible. Let us first consider the text in terms of its meaning: the diadem, a symbol of power, is transferred to the deputies, suggesting a democratization of power. The transfer is not made directly to the Deputies, but to the Deputies' "heads," as if they, in turn, were wearing a multitude of tiny diadems. The word "diadème," however, also designates an insect in the spider family. This permits us to isolate a more tangible meaning which parallels the abstraction of democratization: a spider has spun its web, has delegated its power to its web. The web stands in for the spider or rather is interchangeable with the insect ("un diadème est changé"). The web is thus an extension of the spider through which the latter affirms itself, claims its right to live. In other words, the "diadème" is equivalent to the "mille têtes de députés"; both are of the same nature. The difference lies in the attention given to each: focusing on one causes the other to vanish. Reading "diadème" as "dia-" (through) "-dème" (the people) confirms this assumption. At this point, the entire meaning of the poem becomes concentrated in this segmentation of the word: the "diadème" is changed into "dia-dème," or the "mille têtes de députés" (which make up the "diadème") into "dia-dème."

A similar play guides the demystification of another poem:

Le soleil est en dentelles.

(*12k*; p. 64)

This poem may be read at two levels: at the level of figuration, as in the case of the Apollinaire text analyzed earlier, and at the level of the page. The two levels overlap and say the same thing. As the word "dentelle" (lace) derives from "dent" (tooth), the sentence could evoke an image of the sun drawn by a child who has represented the rays as a "dentelle de dents" around a circle. Another evocation would be even closer to "dentelles": the image of a flower, a daisy for example, surrounded by teeth (the petals). Whether it is a flower on lace or a child's drawing, the sun has been placed at the surface: on cloth or on a piece of paper. In any event, no decision should be made; instead, the different possible evocations should be proliferated in order to avoid imposing a meaning and in order to perceive the surface, a surface spread out "en dentelles" before us, which we must learn to read.

This brings us to the second level of the text: the page. In the absence of a letter inscribed to show the skin, the problem in this case is delicate. Reading the text at the phonemic and graphic levels, we note the repetition of [ã] in "d*en*telles" and in "est *en*." The only difference between [dã] and [tã] is in the voicing; they may be considered as analogous, as repetitious of one another: "le soleil es*t en den*telles." But the repetitions do not end there: on either side of these syllables, the same sounds are propagated almost symmetrically. The [ɛ] of "est" repeats the [ɛ] of "sol*eil*" on one side, and the [ɛ] of "den-t*e*lles" on the other. Further, the graphic "le" is situated at both extremities of the sentence: "*Le* soleil" / "dentel*les*." "Sol-" alone does not enter into the propagation; it is, so to speak, the center (decentered in the text) of the propagation; "sol" is solitary, a unique sun propagating its ray, its doubles, in the sentence.

In spite of those explicit statements on art, poetry, and poetics put forth by Max Jacob (many of which conflict with my thesis, including a claim that art must come from the gut), it can be stated that art for Max Jacob is in the skin, but a skin which—in the absence of *I*—is constituted as a letter. In other words, it is a skin to be taken to the letter. This could be further demonstrated with another poem from "Le Coq et la perle," which in its entirety reads as follows:

Brouillard, étoile d'araignée.

(*12g*; p. 61)

There is no subject, object, or verb; in other words, no message, sender, or receiver. Nothing but a fog ("brouillard"), a canvas ("toile"), a spider's web ("toile d'araignée"), on the surface of which the simple letter "é" of "étoile" (star) has been inscribed to disrupt, to fog up, the message and to render it completely ambiguous: is it a spider in its web? or a star in a fog? Is it a fog *and* a spider's web?[12] The questions could be multiplied, which would only serve to multiply the meanings and thus abolish an only meaning, abolish the direction in which the text may point, or—and this amounts to the same thing—abolish its volume. Nothing remains but a surface without origin, a skin marked as skin by merely a letter. Graphemically, we can also read in "Brouillard *et* toile d'araignée" a mediation between analogues, a repetition of the same. It is worth noting here that the same mediating structure was discerned in "Un diadème est changé en mille têtes de députés," in which "diadème" and "mille têtes de députés" are confused under the mask of "democratization"; and also in "Le soleil est en dentelles," in which two mediating sounds permeated each side of the text. "Brouillard" and "toile d'araignée" both designate a confining density. Further, the similarity between the forms of the star and the spider suggests the possibility of their also being of the same nature. Yet these two serve opposing functions: the star suggests mystery (the astrological mystery of the self) and therefore goodness, whereas the black spider is a barrier, a monster, the evil which prevents the attainment of the star. The mediation therefore serves to confuse the relations between "étoile" and "araignée," which are blurred by the "brouillard" and the "toile d'araignée." The text may thus be conceived of as an at-

12. Similar readings of this poem are found in Annette Thau, "Play with Words and Sounds in the Poetry of Max Jacob," *Revue des lettres modernes*, nos. 336–39 (1975), pp. 125–26.

tempted ascension which aborts because of the confusion caused by the text's own components.

Prose and Verse

This concern with elevation is also found in the following poem, but the methods used are quite different:

> Il n'y a plus rien que le sommet des arbres, il n'y a plus rien que l'arête d'un toit de maison, il n'y a plus rien qu'une fesse malade, plaidant le faux pour savoir le vrai et qui a raison.
>
> (*12e*; p. 58)

Elevation is marked here by the transformation and magnification of the image. In each of the first two clauses, the reader imagines a progression toward an increasingly elevated and increasingly acute peak. The repetition of "il n'y a plus rien que" invites the reader (and the poet) to concentrate on this summit at the expense of the other contents of the canvas. The "plus" of "il n'y a plus rien que" thus acquires two meanings, the first "more and more," the second "nothing but." The third clause appears to present nothing but a grotesque degradation of the initial elevation. It is, in one sense, a degradation, but it may also be conceived of as a third point (in terms of both space and pain) which is even more elevated and acute, pain being more acute than the summit of the trees and the hip of a roof. Considering the position of the sufferer, who is no doubt lying on his stomach with the source of his pain elevated, it is possible to see that this image also forms an acute angle.

The final clause introduces a new turn of events, which the context of *Le Cornet* helps us understand: the doubly elevated buttocks (figuratively and perhaps even literally elevated, as I suggested) make "a false allegation to get at the truth and to know who is right." It is conceivable that courage or modesty prevent the sick person from admitting his pain. But it can also be said that the buttocks are separated by a declivity, like truth from falsehood, and that the subject, like the poet, wears the mask of falsehood in order to know himself, to know the truth about his pain. By donning this mask, he may either transgress truth and become the mask, or acknowledge its falseness. He must therefore decide which is right, the "true" or the "false," in other words, whether he has become the mask or not.

In analyzing the preceding poem, it was necessary to interpolate words such as "point" and "acute" in order to establish the relation between "arête," "sommet," and "fesse," and to read the text. In the next poem, one of the rare verse poems in *Le Cornet*, there are no missing elements. The poet selects three words almost at random and develops a series of associations between them:

> Quelques fois, un poisson nageant
> Aux vagues montre un ventre blanc
> L'aérostat, poisson volant,
> Parfois s'offre blanc au nuage,
> La danseuse, se retournant,
> Montre en scène à tous les étages
> Un dos poisseux de diamants.
>
> (*12m*; pp. 68–69)

The three randomly selected terms are "fish," "airship," and "dancer." The intent is to bring them as close together as is possible in a single text. This verse poem has the same structure as "l'enfant, l'éfant, . . . " with the exception that, here, the relations between the enumerated terms are provided. The poem is thus much less distant from the reader in that he is not obliged to supply any extratextual terms or ideas. The relation between the three terms is based on the use of analogous images in different contexts. Like a flying fish, the moon (the airship) may be seen through the clouds, and, like the fish and the moon, the dancer reveals "a back slimy [poisseux] with diamonds." "Poisseux" echoes "poisson," and "diamonds" recall "airship" because of their association with stars.

The poem, however, goes considerably beyond a simple association of randomly selected terms because, on the one hand, the poet succeeds in establishing a complete identity between the three elements and, on the other hand, this identity (which is also a metamorphosis) provokes a certain uneasiness. The first instance of taking an element beyond its natural confines is fairly straightforward: in the first two lines, the swimming fish is also a kind of flying fish because it is able to leave the water and reveal its white underbelly. In the next two lines, the airship becomes the previously suggested flying fish, or rather the moon is both moon and flying fish, thereby establishing a further identity between the waves and the clouds (which, incidentally, may have the same form). Consequently, the dancer, who is also a moon-fish, like them reveals her back to "the entire audience" ("tous les étages") or to the cloud-waves. The synthesis of the three elements is simultaneously a metamorphosis, since the freshness of the fish and the serenity of the moon both become viscous: the discomfort of the sweating dancer. The diamonds on her back are fake; they are beads of sweat (the same beads which, on the fish, would designate freshness) which form in spite of her, while she supposedly dances to evoke a fish or the moon. Like the poet, the dancer is trying to be something other than what she is; she succeeds up to a point but, as soon as she turns her back, her true self is revealed, a being soaked in anguish, straining to play yet unable to conceal her efforts to play.

The fact that this poem is in verse and less "enigmatic" than the preceding ones (because the relations between the terms are provided) could be explained in reference to some of the theories concerning prose poems that Max Jacob stated in the Preface. I have shown that prose poems must meet two requirements: one situational (the margin, the distancing of the reader), the other stylistic (textual construction). This verse poem, perhaps because it is in verse, conforms to only one of these laws. It has style yet is not situated. It is well constructed; the relations between "poisson," "aérostat," and "danseuse" are given and serve to unify the poem, but it is not situated, precisely because these relations are given and do not have to be established by the reader.

This poem could be contrasted with "La Mendiante de Naples," in which the reader participates more actively:

> Quand j'habitais Naples, il y avait à la porte de mon palais une mendiante à laquelle je jetais des pièces de monnaie avant de monter en voiture. Un jour, surpris de n'avoir jamais de remerciements, je regardai la mendiante. Or, comme je regardais, je vis que ce que j'avais pris pour une mendiante, c'était une caisse de bois peinte en vert qui contenait de la terre rouge et quelques bananes à demi-pourries . . .
>
> (*39*; p. 144)

We can imagine that the poet gave coins over a period of time to what he took to be a beggar woman. As soon as he notices that the exchange is one-sided, that he has received no thanks, he realizes that he has been mistaking a wooden crate for a beggar woman. The ease with which he had made this mistake indicates that there must have been a close relation between the two, a relation such that they were considered identical until the moment when the poet recognized the inequality of the exchange and separated the two compared objects.

What he had taken for a beggar woman has four colors: green, red, yellow, and grey—the last because the yellow bananas were half-rotten, and hence half-grey. There is a dessert called "the four beggars," composed of four types of fruit: figs, almonds, chestnuts, and grapes. The dessert is given this name because the color of each fruit is the same as that of the robe worn by each of the mendicant orders: Franciscan, Dominican, Carmelite, and Augustinian. The relation between the beggar woman and the crate may be understood in the same way: just as each of the mendicant orders is represented by the color of a fruit, so is the beggar woman in the poem represented by the four-colored crate (the rotten bananas being a perfect indication of her penury). Therefore, if the poet receives no gratitude in exchange for his alms, it is because his money is destined to God, by association with the mendicant orders, and God never gives thanks. From this point of view, the haughty mood of the poet leaving his palace is upset when he recognizes the inequality of the exchange, for he shall henceforth give alms not out of generosity but with humility.

In this prose poem, the reader had to supply the idea of the four-beggars dessert in order to read it. It should be noted that the element brought by the reader is not foreign to the poem; it is not a structure admitted a priori which we impose on the poem, but rather an element implicitly dictated by the poem itself. In other words, the solution to the riddle is imprisoned in the poem, and the reader's role consists of releasing it in order to understand the poem through it. There is, in fact, a kind of superimposition of two discourses, one of which generates the other.

In "La Clef" the reader follows the same steps in reaching an understanding of the poem, but in this case the vehicle unifying the poem is a well-known cliché:

> Quand le sire de Framboisy revint de guerre, sa femme lui fit de grands reproches à l'église, alors il dit: "Madame, voici la clef de tous mes biens, je pars pour jamais." La dame laissa tomber la clef sur le pavé du temple par délicatesse. Une nonne, dans un coin, priait, parce qu'elle avait égaré la sienne, la clef du couvent et qu'on n'y pouvait pas entrer. "Voyez donc si votre serrure s'accommode de celle-ci." Mais la clef n'était plus là. Elle était déjà au musée de Cluny: c'était une énorme clef en forme de tronc d'arbre.
>
> (*35*; p. 114)

Anything is possible in this mysterious medieval atmosphere. When the Lord of Framboisy gives his wife the key to all his goods, he takes "la clef des champs" (that is, he escapes) in exchange, thereby freeing himself and his goods. It must be noted that it is only by surrendering the key, by ridding himself of it, that he can free himself. The key thus becomes the symbol of enslavement, as it confines its owner and becomes, in a certain fashion, his mistress. It is evident that the cliché "prendre la clef des champs" is completely reversed, because in this poem, taking the key means becoming a prisoner. For this reason the lord's wife "modestly" drops the key; she intuits its erotic meaning and tries to get rid of it. We can also say that the nun, who is free because she cannot enter the convent, refuses the key in order not to be imprisoned. The only way for all to keep their freedom is to lock up the key itself, which is precisely why it ends up in the Cluny Museum, that famous museum of medieval art where relics, such as this enormous erotic key which becomes its owner's mistress, are displayed. In the museum, the key becomes a burlesque work of art which never leaves its case, in very much the same way as the ludic poems in this collection are confined to the dice cup.

Max Jacob often states the riddle and supplies its solution. The reader's task in these cases consists of finding the relations between the riddle and the solution. In "Capitale. Tapis de table," for example, the riddle is stated in the title in the form of a juxtaposition of two expressions which have no apparent semantic connection with one another. The terms do stand in a certain phonetic relation to one another (minor syllabic alterations permit the derivation of "tapis de table" from "capitale"), but the question of establishing a link between them based on their significations still remains unresolved. The text, which should provide the answer, therefore represents a solution to both the riddle and the disparity between the two terms:

> Capitale. Tapis de table
> La petite a les seins trop écartés, il faut soigner cela à Paris: plus tard, ce serait vulgaire. Mais, à Paris, toutes les boutiques se ressemblent: or et cristal: médecin des chapeaux! Médecin des montres! où est le médecin des seins?
>
> (*40*; p. 146)

We can imagine a bourgeois family from the provinces arriving in Paris where conformity is the rule. The family realizes that, once in the capital, the little girl will be singled out as having a physical defect which, in the provinces, would have gone unnoticed. The defect thus becomes the family's topic of conversation; in other words, it is put on the table ("mis sur le tapis de table") because they are in the capital. The poem, however, goes beyond this simple wordplay for, now that the "little one" is in Paris and has had her defect recognized, she is the center of attention in the family, and thus subject to considerable discomfort, especially when her physique is spoken of and passed around at the table like playing cards. Her breasts have become objects which do not function properly and which must be seen to by a doctor.

Because the breasts are treated as ornaments by the family, it is natural that they should think of the shops which specialize in this phenomenon, the shops which market appearance: "gold and crystal." But the little one has no need for this kind of embellishment; she needs a "médecin"—which should also be read as "mes deux seins." They find a hat doctor (a specialist in objects which grotesquely resemble breasts) and a watch doctor, "médecin des montres," because showing her off ("la montrer") motivates their seeking a doctor, but they never find a "médecin" who specializes in "seins" as his name implies. The young girl's torment continues because her breasts remain the object and subject of the conversation in the capital.

What is a reading of the surface? I am evidently not referring to the Chomskian distinction between deep structure and surface structure, in which the surface structure is understood in terms of deep structure. In fact, it is only through the text's own abolition of its depth that we have become aware of the surface of Max Jacob's poems. Surface reading implies two things: reading the surface in the sense of perceiving or isolating it, but also reading it at its own level. Reading the surface would entail abstracting one's own volume, spreading oneself thin to see the words and letters. A reading of the surface is also in the singular: there are not several skins, but one; multiplicity goes with volume. In this sense, the uniqueness of the surface is inversely related to the uniqueness of the subject. The subject implies grounding and depth, whereas the surface implies a multiplicity of subjects, all situated at the same level, with neither foundation nor depth. Deciphering Max Jacob's riddles entails precisely an awareness of that surface: recognizing it and deriving a reading from it. Each poem is a new surface, a new riddle to recognize and read; each poem, a new mask to recognize and read.

In concluding this chapter, I would like to quote a remark made in 1933 by Marcel Raymond on Max Jacob's poetry. It sums up many of my claims: "Neither we nor the author ever know [the poems'] identity. Similarly, his universe deceives us, . . . we never grasp what 'it means to say.'"[13] If we never grasp what Max Jacob's poems mean to say, all the better. This lack has taught us to see all the more.

13. *De Baudelaire au Surréalisme* (1933; rpt. Paris: Corti, 1952), pp. 254–55. My translation.

6 ⬡

Parodies

Legrandin

Marcel Proust's Legrandin as he appears in the first pages of *À la recherche du temps perdu* will serve as a figure for the discussion of parody in *Le Cornet à dés*. As Legrandin's name indicates, he is evidently split, both large and small (*Legrand*: the big one, *-in*, a diminutive), two profiles for two different identities. In one profile, presented to the chatelaine, we can read the signs of grandeur, which come naturally. Yet this lack of affectation is conscious, exaggerated, and strained, quite unlike Swann's. Simultaneously, the other side, offered to Marcel and his father, contains, parallel to the first, an expression of duplicity entirely localized in a look in which "il subtilisa les finesses de l'amabilité jusqu'aux clignements de la connivence, aux *demi-mots*, aux *sous-entendus*, au mystère de la complicité, et finalement exalta les assurances d'amitiés jusqu'aux *protestations* de tendresse, jusqu'à la *déclaration* d'amour"[1] (my italics). Another grossly exaggerated false image.

Legrandin is entirely other than himself: he proffers only profiles; at the same time, he is completely himself, for Legrandin *is* no one but these two separate profiles, each defined with regard to the other and not with regard to a "self." Here the dialectic of being and seeming, of interior and exterior, collapses; the reader, Marcel, and even Legrandin himself cannot locate his "interior." Legrandin, as subject, tends to disappear. The relevance of this example is that it serves to clarify the manner in which such disappearances occur; in other words, the way in which otherness is composed. I speak of composition because, looking closely at the italicized words in the Proust quotation, we can observe that the profile is a discourse (Marcel's grandmother even says that Legrandin talks too much like a book), a true parody—that is, a text made along the lines of, yet separate from, another one, a text carefully and consciously composed, an exaggeration which marks its own falseness. In this case it is a parody of a text which might have existed, which might have said: "I am truly one of you," but which, in fact, does not exist. Legrandin's expression is in effect an otherness without origin.

M. de Max

> M. de Max offrait tous ses profils à chacun des deux partis comme autant de prismes géants.
>
> (*12o*; p. 72)

---

1. "He subtilized the refinements of congeniality to the winkings of connivance, to *half-words*, to *hints*, to the mysteries of complicity, and finally he exalted the assurances of friendship to *protestations* of tenderness, to the *declaration* of love." (*Du côté de chez Swann* [1913; rpt. Paris: Gallimard, Collection de Poche, 1954], p. 151.) My translation and my italics.

The difference between M. Legrandin and M. de Max is strictly quantitative—yet this distinction is a capital one, since it gives otherness a completely different configuration. M. de Max has not two but a multiplicity of profiles. Further, he does not differentiate between the parts: he offers all his profiles to all sides. This is not to suggest, however, that otherness and separation have been eliminated, because he still presents profiles, other sides of "himself." It is only that the other is now generalized, undifferentiated, and thereby constantly undermined, leaving only otherness in all its superficiality: something other than himself is put forth, a multiplicity of selves which affirm the nonexistence of a unified, underlying self, yet which nevertheless constitute the sole "self."

Modern linguistics has shown that the production of meaning is based on the principle of difference (the difference between two phonemes, for example, gives each its value) and that, without this difference, communication, which is to say exchange (giving—or offering, like M. de Max—and taking), would be impossible: each word would have the same value, and there would be, to borrow an expression from Georges Bataille, a general rather than a restrained economy. The latter, based upon difference, generates reserves and subsequently establishes value. When there are no reserves, nothing hidden, no interior and no origin, difference and ultimately the subject (the "self") are caught up in play which borders on lack of meaning.

The question of origins and meaning is precisely the ground upon which Max Jacob differentiates between his work and that of his predecessor Aloysius Bertrand. He criticized Bertrand's "romantisme à la manière de Callot," which, as he says, "attachant l'attention à des couleurs trop violentes, voile l'œuvre même" ("Préface de 1916," *1*; p. 23). His statement should not be taken as a condemnation of parody; Max Jacob would be the last to do so, his own work being almost exclusively composed, as I have suggested earlier, of parodies, pastiches, and caricatures, all of which he explicitly ac-

knowledges as such. It is not Bertrand's "à la manière de" that
he criticizes, but rather the fact that his imitation is focused,
that it points explicitly toward its origin, that this indication
(this "meaning") eclipses the second text—Bertrand's own—
and reveals the model.

Max Jacob's parody seeks to conceal its source while claim-
ing to be secondary, fictitious, a spurious copy announcing its
falseness in regard to an origin, but an origin crossed-out,
eclipsed, and at times even nonexistent. His parody is a falsehood, an artifice independent of what it might have imitated
or what it does imitate; the text artificially (with art) makes
itself unrecognizable—it institutes what Max Jacob calls in his
Preface a "margin." In this schema, the poet feeds off his own
illusion; with parody (the parallel ode), in the generalized
sense in which I have described it, he pretends to be able to
escape his confining state, the prison where he is neither
player nor poet, the prison of non-presence. He pretends to
escape by appropriating the mode of the "other's" play—
"other's" in quotes because the text seeks to undermine the
origin of that otherness and not otherness itself, since the
latter is, at least in this case, the foundation of presence.

The moment of presence is not destined to last (how could
it materially last beyond the reading of the text?). It begins to
shrink once the reading is undertaken: as the poem spreads
out before the reader's eyes, it simultaneously presents its
otherness, and the poet, who sought to settle in the material-
ity of his mask, is little by little unmasked by that very awareness. Whence the search for another mask, another parody,
or for a parodied parody, a movement toward an exteriority
which is always more inaccessible, always more scenic, more
radically other and always destined to fail.

Identities

Augustine était fille de ferme quand le Président la remar-
qua. Pour éviter le scandale, il lui décerna des titres et des
brevets d'institutrice, puis un "de" vers son nom, quelque ar-

gent, et plus il la pourvoyait, plus elle était digne de lui. Je me suis tout donné à moi-même, pauvre paysan breton, le titre de duc, le droit de porter un monocle, j'ai pu grandir ma taille, ma pensée et je ne pourrai pas être digne de moi-même.

(*12d*; p. 57)

This text is a fairy tale, albeit an elliptical and "modern" (democratized) one: a president/prince charming notices a peasant girl, falls in love with her, and changes her into a first lady/princess. But there is no magic (wave of the wand) in this passage from peasant to princess; it has to be worked at, especially from the exterior: titles, and a "de" before her name. In other words, the peasant's value has to be raised; she has to be supplemented by a series of signifiers, made into a text denoting dignity.

This text, however, does not work in a single direction; it also serves to reflect the bestowed image on the one conferring it, for what the president ultimately wants is for the peasant to be worthy of him, meaning for her to help him maintain his president's image. In a sense, the president gives her what he feels *he* is due. The "poor Breton peasant," the poet, taking the example of the fairy tale (which, like all fairy tales, has a happy ending) bestows a similar system of signifiers on himself, such as the title of duke, a monocle, expanded stature and thought in order to be this other person, in order to see himself in another way and to be worthy of himself. But, as the bequest is purely reflexive (he gives himself to himself and not through an intermediary), implying an awareness of the bequest and especially of its ends, the metamorphosis does not occur, and neither otherness nor dignity is attained. It is as if the poet still saw the poor Breton peasant through the mirror-text which he has fabricated for himself. Whether that text is the one which the president fabricates, or which the poor Breton peasant/poet fabricates, or whether it is this very poem in the form of a fairy tale that is a parody made at a distance, with "style," to use Max Jacob's expression, it intentionally invites otherness. This movement toward the other is destined, however, to fail because of the short-circuited exchange which generates self-consciousness and self-knowledge.

La Vraie Ruine

Quand j'étais jeune, je croyais que les génies et les fées s'étaient dérangés pour me guider et quelle que fût l'injure qu'on m'adressât, je croyais qu'on soufflait aux autres des mots qui n'avaient en but que mon bien et le mien seul. La réalité et le désastre qui m'ont fait chanteur sur cette place m'apprennent que j'ai toujours été abandonné des dieux. O génies, ô fées! rendez-moi aujourd'hui mon illusion.

(43; p. 182)

The young poet's beliefs bear a striking resemblance to what the romantics have called "poetic inspiration," but of course it is exaggerated here: spirits and fairies whisper words and guide beleaguered poets. For the romantics, the question of the subject is, so to speak, settled in advance: chosen and guided, they know that they are worthy of the gods, that they belong to them.

Max Jacob's aged and disillusioned poet realizes that his situation is quite different. He is no longer a poet-magus, but "a singer in this square." He has, so to speak, fallen from poet to singer, a singer seen and heard on a square. He realizes that he has always been ignored by the gods, that he is earthbound and that his beliefs were self-deceptions. In the last sentence he begs the spirits and fairies to give him back his illusions so that he may again be among the chosen; symptomatically and no doubt nostalgically, his invocation is in romantic style: he uses the traditional "Ô . . . , ô . . . ," exclamation which, given his sudden change of tone, borders here on caricature. Restoring his illusions means forgetting his earthly situation; it means pretending that he has not fallen, that the origin has not been lost and that communication is still possible. We must nevertheless insist that the earthbound poet is aware that the illusion is actually a temporary disguise, a parody, reminiscent of Rimbaud's biographical summary style in "Une Saison en enfer"—a parody which never quite permits the parodied object to be attained, and which sooner or later brings the poet back to "reality and disaster."

Counterfeit

> Fausses Nouvelles! Fosses nouvelles!
>
> A une représentation de *Pour la Couronne*, à l'Opéra, quand Desdémone chante "Mon père est à Goritz et mon coeur à Paris", on a entendu un coup de feu dans une loge de cinquième galerie, puis un second aux fauteuils et instantanément des échelles de cordes se sont déroulées; un homme a voulu descendre des combles: une balle l'a arrêté à la hauteur du balcon. Tous les spectateurs étaient armés et il s'est trouvé que la salle n'était pleine que de . . . et de . . . Alors, il y a eu des assassinats du voisin, des jets de pétrole enflammé. Il y a eu des sièges de loges, le siège de la scène, le siège d'un strapontin et cette bataille a duré dix-huit jours. On a peut-être ravitaillé les deux camps, je ne sais, mais ce que je sais fort bien c'est que les journalistes sont venus pour un si horrible spectacle, que l'un d'eux étant souffrant, y a envoyé madame sa mère et que celle-ci a été beaucoup intéressée par le sang-froid d'un jeune gentilhomme français qui a tenu dix-huit jours dans une avant-scène sans rien prendre qu'un peu de bouillon. Cet épisode de la guerre des Balcons a beaucoup fait pour les engagements volontaires en province. Et je sais, au bord de ma rivière, sous mes arbres, trois frères en uniformes tout neufs qui se sont embrassés les yeux secs, tandis que leurs familles cherchaient des tricots dans les armoires des mansardes.
>
> (5, pp. 30–31)

The title of this poem could be taken as the shout of a newspaper seller, anxious to sell the latest news, who paradoxically proclaims that the news which he sells is inherently false, and hence not worth reading. Yet the news exists, the text is there and someone reads it. Someone buys the paper in spite of the seller's announcement. It is possible therefore that the buyer understood "fosses nouvelles" (new graves) instead of "fausses nouvelles" (false news). In any case, the reader is not disappointed for, behind the façade of newspaper reporting, there is a theater implying fictitiousness and a war inside the theater, on and off stage, and finally a real war which creates new graves.

The warring in the theater is touched off by the action on stage where an opera, with both poetic and warlike connotations, *Pour la Couronne*, is being performed. The play triggers a battle of gargantuan proportions, communicated not only through the exploits of the combatants who kill one another, burn right and left, and do battle for eighteen days without fresh supplies, but also through its vocabulary: "Il y a eu des sièges de loge, le siège de la scène et le siège d'un strapontin," an abundance of wordplay worthy of Rabelais. The comic exaggerations confirm the falseness of the news, but this does not prevent the news from creating "fosses nouvelles," for, in the last line, there clearly is a real war going on, one no longer set in the "balcons," but perhaps in the "Balkans," with the families of the three brothers looking for sweaters to help them endure the cold of that region.

From this we can see how Max Jacob, intending to write a parody, a kind of journalistic account of "false news," transforms his parody, goes beyond it and creates a new poem. The parody served him only as an extraliterary mask to mystify the reader who, expecting to read a poem, finds instead a news item. The reader is thereby "situated" with regard to the poem; but, when he studies it, he goes beyond the mask to bring to light a reality with tragic consequences.

In "Latude-l'étude," Max Jacob makes use of a mode which is closely related to poetry, that of erudite scholarship:

> On a beaucoup écrit sur le cas de Latude, on n'a pas écrit la vérité. C'est pour se défendre contre son propre coeur que Mme de Pompadour, ce gracieux Napoléon de l'amour, fit enfermer à la Bastille le petit officier bleu et blanc. Latude s'évade! où va-t-il? au pays de Spinoza. Mais il comprit que le goût de la méditation ne se satisfait que dans les tours et il revint à son écrin d'amour.
>
> (*46*; p. 207)

The tone of the first sentence indicates that this is a kind of study being conducted on Latude, an adventurer who spent thirty-five years in prison for his repeated plotting against Mme de Pompadour. This first sentence could be found in virtually any historical essay tinted with polemic, but it takes a poetic turn when we consider the exaggerated, almost clumsy internal rhymes of the title, of "Pompadour"/"amour," and of "écrit"/"écrin." Latude is in fact the poet who, because he writes, ("écrit"), ends up in an "écrin," and the study in question is a search for his identity. The impersonal "on" (one) thus becomes the poet who "has not written the truth" about himself and who is reconsidering his position. He finds that his beloved, the Pompadour, is a kind of general who takes military steps to "protect herself against her own heart." She locks up the poet, who is nothing but a petty officer, a malleable object. When he escapes, he flees to Spinoza's country, which is to say to rationalism and the clarity of a prosaic mode. In a manner of speaking, he frees himself from poetry itself, but his freedom is short-lived, for he returns to his tower and reassumes the role of the blue-and-white object which his mistress keeps locked in a jewel case. He returns to his prison because it is there that he can meditate, there that he can become a poet.

Tautologies

In "Roman feuilleton" the uncovering of a system of exchange gives a meaning to the whirlwind of similar terms:

> Donc, une auto s'arrêta devant l'hôtel à Chartres. Savoir qui était dans cette auto, devant cet hôtel, si c'était Toto, si c'était Totel, voilà ce que vous voudriez savoir, mais vous ne le saurez jamais ... jamais ... La fréquentation des Parisiens a fait beaucoup de bien aux hôteliers de Chartres, mais la fréquentation des hôteliers de Chartres a fait beaucoup de mal aux Parisiens pour certaines raisons. Un garçon d'hôtel prit les bottes du propriétaire de l'auto et les cira: ces bottes furent mal cirées, car l'abondance des autos dans les hôtels empêchait les domestiques de prendre les dispositions nécessaires à un bon cirage de bottes; fort heureusement, la même abondance empêcha notre héros d'apercevoir que ses bottes étaient mal

cirées. Que venait faire notre héros dans cette vieille cité de Chartres, qui est si connue? il venait chercher un médecin, parce qu'il n'y en a pas assez à Paris pour le nombre de maladies qu'il avait.

(25; p. 93)

This poem may be read as a parody of serial novels. It could be said that Max Jacob is caricaturing the complexities of plot and the abundance of poorly developed characters, many of whom (like Toto and Totel) are virtually indistinguishable. Even the objects in the "novel" are poorly defined; there are "autos" and "hotels" (the phonic resemblance of which must be stressed) which are not unlike Toto and Totel. In short, both characters and object constitute incomprehensible *tauto*logies (a word which Max Jacob might well have had in mind while composing this poem). Nevertheless, the incomprehensible parody is only the mask; it is the surface of the poem and the mode which the poet has adopted to situate both himself and his poem. And, like all masks, it is destined to come off. Let us take the difference between Toto and Totel seriously, let us say that these truly are two different characters (or different words). This distinction permits the establishment of others:

Toto	Totel
Auto	Hotel
Parisiens (owners of cars)	Hoteliers (owners of hotels)
Parisians benefit hostelers	Hostelers harm Parisians

  Abundance of autos in the hotels
  Abundance of good in evil
  Abundance of illnesses in the hero

It is clear from this outline that if a distinction is attempted between Toto and Totel, it is soon destroyed, not only in appearance—by the resemblance between the two names and by the progression from single to double to numerous—but also *in fact*, since the good, associated with autos and hence with Toto, blends with the harm associated with hotels and

Totel, and vice versa. Thus, the reason why we will never know whether it was Toto or Totel who came to Chartres is that the two are one. The hero, this Toto-Totel, goes to the hotel with his ailments; he brings good, but in exchange receives only harm covered over with a slight superficial benefit: the poorly polished boots. In other words, the care which he sought in Chartres, the site of his pilgrimage (which might suggest a further play between "hôtel" and "autel" [altar]), is only polish, a superficial good which temporarily assuages his suffering. Once again, Max Jacob provides within the poem the key to its understanding: like the poorly polished boots, the poem is coated with a parody which allows a persistent agony to show through.

In "Un Peu de critique d'art" Max Jacob distorts the mode of critical biography to comic extremes:

> Jacques Claès est vraiment un nom de peintre hollandais. Jetons, si vous le voulez bien, un coup d'œil sur ses origines. La mère du petit Jacques se pâlissait le visage avec du vinaigre, comme elle l'a avoué elle-même, c'est ce qui explique pourquoi les tableaux du maître ont l'air vernis. Dans le village de Jacques, le jour de la Saint-Couvreur, c'était l'usage que les couvreurs de toitures se laissâssent tomber du haut des toits sans écraser les passants, ils devaient aussi jeter des cordes du trottoir aux cheminées. Ensemble très pittoresque qui, certainement, a dû donner à notre peintre le goût du pittoresque.
>
> (22; p. 87)

At first, this poem appears extremely logical. The title invites the reader to consider the text not as a poem, but as a piece of rational criticism. This rationalism is sustained with the help of unliterary expressions, such as "vraiment," "jetons un coup d'œil," "le petit Jacques," etc.; literary or technical expressions, such as "nom de peintre" (with implicit reference to "nom de plume"), "se laissâssent" (the use of the imperfect subjunctive), "ensemble pittoresque," "goût du pittoresque," etc.; and a language of cause and effect, such as "c'est ce qui explique." Despite this logical appearance, the poem has a certain disconcerting quality. We perceive a lack of con-

tinuity between the title and the text: the reader expects art
criticism, yet finds criticism of an artist; he then realizes that
this is not even a mockery of the biographical type of criticism
that criticizes the man instead of his work, for it is only a
criticism of an artist's name—the poem states "Jacques Claès
is truly a name . . . Let's . . . look into its origins." The research is both superfluous and gratuitous because we can tell
from the beginning that the name is Dutch. It appears further that a comparable tautological effect is maintained
throughout this logically formed poem. When we respond to
the invitation to look at the origins of the name, we note that
the search leads to the mother, which is hardly surprising,
considering that it was she who gave him the name. The tautology continues with "ensemble très pittoresque qui a cer-
tainement dû donner à notre peintre le goût du pittoresque."
But, here, the tautology takes on a different character; it becomes speciously explicit and thus mocks itself; the repetition
of the word "pittoresque" is the only connection between the
painter and his painting.

The poem nevertheless is composed of two movements in
opposite directions. The first consists of a series of "layers,"
each of which serves to cover the preceding one. These layers
take the form of words or expressions which cover, so to
speak, those preceding them, thus masking them: "Jacques
Claès" is displaced by "nom de peintre," in turn obscured by
"mère," and so on to "goût du pittoresque," passing through
"vinaigre," "vernis," "les couvreurs de toitures qui se laissâssent
tomber," and "ensemble pittoresque." Groping to explain the
painting through the origin of the name, the "art critic" began with the name and ended with the insignificant "goût du
pittoresque," which explains nothing.

The second movement, as absurd as the first, goes in the
opposite direction. It is based upon the well-known cliché
"like father, like son," transformed by Max Jacob into "like
mother, like son," which is implicit throughout the poem.
Since the mother whitened her face with vinegar, she gave
birth to one who "whitens" canvas: a painter. The latter, having a hereditary taste for whitening, composes (gives birth to)

canvases which have a "*var*nished (*vernis*) appearance" (just like mother's *v*inegar [*vinaigre*]), and which represent "couvreurs" who "throw themselves from the rooftops without crushing the pedestrians," which is to say, with art, like their master. The reader may push the hereditary succession one step in either direction: the poet, himself a kind of "couvreur," is necessarily the father of this all-covering poem coated with a layer of parody; on the other hand, there is the critic who disregards the canvas and covers it with such words as "ensemble pittoresque" in order to explain it. Furthermore, these two contrary movements are symbolized by the "couvreurs" who throw themselves from the roof and who "were also expected to throw ropes from the sidewalks to the chimneys."

Self-Parody

"L'Art Ariste" may be thought of as a triple parody: of newspaper reporting, the realistic novel, and Max Jacob's poetry:

> Le journal *Fémina* décrit l'hôtel de la duchesse d'H . . . comme une bâtisse fort triste et s'attarde à dépeindre en rouge gris le pavé de la cour. Il dit que la chambre centrale est habitée par un vieux domestique qui veille sur l'hôtel, l'été. Ce qui l'étonne, c'est que les rideaux traînent toujours un peu à terre comme une robe à queue et il confesse que, faisant luimême des romans, il a tout regardé avec soin et même les autres hôtels du voisinage où les rideaux traînent aussi à terre. Il a été témoin d'une scène ou demi-scène de la fille avec la mère à propos de physique ou de fusil, la bonne ayant demandé si on faisait beaucoup de physique ou de fusil dans le pensionnat où on envoyait son fils à elle. Il y eut une gifle appliquée comme une certaine feuille ronde pareille au cresson et qui pousse sur les murs. J'ai parlé du domestique qui garde l'hôtel, l'été. C'est ce domestique qui est chargé de la vidange. La duchesse a un profil aristocratique et la plante de la muraille s'appelle aristoloche, l'auteur du reportage s'appelle Aristide.

(37, p. 122)

This text, written in the form of a newspaper article, insists upon objectivity. At the beginning of the poem, for example, neither an author nor an impersonal "on" is credited with describing the hotel, but rather the newspaper itself, as if the newspaper alone had prepared the review. Naturally, phrases such as "Le journal *Fémina* décrit" and "s'attarde à dépeindre" could be considered figures of speech comparable to "the newspaper is conducting an investigation." But when we learn that the newspaper "is astonished," that it "confesses," and that it "writes novels itself," the figures of speech take on another value: on the one hand they create a comic effect, and on the other they reinforce the idea that the reporting is objective because it is done by an object, the newspaper. This concern for objectivity is carried even further by the re-porter-newspaper's efforts to present detailed descriptions: "il s'attarde à dépeindre en rouge gris le pavé de la cour." It also seeks to establish generalities which might provide some insight into the way things are done in the particular neigh-borhood: "il a tout regardé avec soin et même les autres hôtels du voisinage où les rideaux trainent aussi à terre." This newspaper is, in effect, a bona fide Balzac who studies the intended objects of its descriptions with care and then recre-ates them as faithfully as possible.

Furthermore, as is often the case in Balzac's novels, the ob-jects in the hotel bear a certain resemblance to those who in-habit it: "les Rideaux traînent toujours un peu à terre comme une robe à queue," perhaps even like the train of the gown worn by the noble duchess. It is therefore not surprising to learn at the end of the poem that the author of the article is called Aristides, the same as the Greek general nicknamed the Just. The title could thus be read as "L'Art d'Aristide," in other words "l'art réaliste," which is paragrammatically con-tained in "L'Art Ariste." Aristides the Just remains faithful to his objectivity: when he witnesses a scene in the hotel, he cor-rects himself and says that it was instead a half-scene, as it appears that he only saw part of it; he knows that it had to do with "physique ou fusil" and that someone had been slapped. The reader could interpolate the other "half-scene": "physique" and "fusil" have erotic connotations: the maid's son is exiled to a boarding school, and perhaps she fears that he will get involved with "physique" or "fusil" while he is there. It could thus be inferred that the mother and the daughter are arguing because the daughter has had an affair with the maid's son. This is naturally reminiscent of the realistic novel: a maid's son dreams of entering into high society by seducing the daughter of a duchess, and so on.

At the end of the poem, the realistic art of reporting and novel writing is transformed into "L'Art Ariste" of Max Jacob for, as Suzanne Bernard points out, the intent is to proliferate words with the root "ariste."[2] This serves to confer a unity on the various details of the realistic text, a unity also imposed through the phonic resemblance between the details and the images presented in the text. The phrase "gifle appliquée comme une certaine feuille ronde pareille au cresson et qui pousse sur les murs" is reiterated in the aristocratic profile of the duchess, as a slap (gifle) is generally administered to a face, and by the round-leaved (feuille ronde) aristolochia. The result is a kind of surrealist sculpture which depicts a profile with a flower on its cheek in the guise of a slap; a sculpture which sums up and, at the same time, fixes the anecdote.

In "Le Cygne (genre essai plein d'esprit)" Max Jacob covertly parodies another type of criticism: the criticism which his reader must engage in to understand his poetry:

> Le cygne se chasse en Allemagne, patrie de Lohengrin. Il sert de marque à un faux col dans les pissotières. Sur les lacs, on le confond avec les fleurs et on s'extasie, alors, sur sa forme de bateau; d'ailleurs, on le tue impitoyablement pour le faire chanter. La peinture utiliserait volontiers le cygne, mais nous n'avons plus de peinture. Quand il a eu le temps de se changer en femme avant de mourir, sa chair est moins dure que dans le cas contraire: les chasseurs l'estiment davantage alors. Sous le nom d'eider, les cygnes aidèrent à l'édredon. Et cela ne lui

---

2. *Le Poème en prose de Baudelaire à nos jours* (Paris: Nizet, 1953), p. 633.

va pas mal. On appelle hommes-cygnes ou hommes insignes les hommes qui ont le cou long comme Fénelon, cygne de Cambrai. Etc.

(26; p. 95)

Like Mallarmé and Baudelaire before him, Max Jacob is intent upon writing his poem about the swan.[3] It is worth recalling that, to his symbolist precursors, the swan was the symbol of the poet, either alienated in his environment (Baudelaire) or deprived of poetic ability (Mallarmé: "Le vierge, le vivace . . . "). In keeping with this tradition, Max Jacob presents all the elements commonly associated with swans. Referring perhaps to Baudelaire, he says that "the swan is hunted in Germany, the homeland of Lohengrin." The fact that the swan changes into a woman could also be an allusion to Baudelaire's "Le Cygne," in which Andromache shares the poet's exile. An allusion to Mallarmé might be found in "they mercilessly kill it to hear its song," which, on a certain level, conveys the suffering associated with creativity. This poem also contains an allusion to a short story by Villiers de l'Îsle-Adam titled "Le Tueur de cygnes,"[4] which has an epigraph attributed to Hugo: "Les cygnes comprennent les signs" (*sic*). Not only does Max Jacob repeat this play on words, but he also makes use of the association between the poet and the swan, and the idea that the swan sings before his death.

This poem is in the form of a short essay, very like one which might be found in an encyclopedia under the entry "Swan," in which the gamut of significations and connotations would be given. These allusions to Baudelaire, Mallarmé, and Villiers de l'Îsle-Adam constitute only a portion of the "encyclopedia." In this form, the poem becomes a parody of itself; we can imagine the poet, intent upon writing a poem about the swan, going to an encyclopedia for information which he will try to organize into a poem. The poem also

3. Note that whereas Judith Morganroth Schneider translated "cygne" as "cygnet" in order to retain the idea of "sign," I have chosen "swan," which preserves the implications of the song of the swan, etc.

4. *Tribulat Bonhomet* (Paris: 1887), p. 3.

constitutes a parody of the "genre essai plein d'esprit," the kind the reader will have to write in order to demystify the poem, for he too must turn to a dictionary to find the different connotations of the word "swan." The poem may therefore be considered on several levels: as a poem entitled "Le Cygne," as a poem parodying this poem, as an essay on the poem, and as a parody of that essay.

The poet thus recognizes the reader's play and shows him what it consists of, in the same manner that the reader exposes the poet's play. The game is settled in advance: it will end in a draw. We therefore have nothing to lose by pushing it to that point: the swan is a game bird, a means of transportation for Lohengrin, and a mark (a sign) "à un faux col dans les pissotières," which might also be read as a "faux col à un bock de bière," because of the homonymy and because the expression "faux col" is usually associated with beer. It functions as a metaphor in poetry when taken for a flower or a boat. It may also be used in the expression "swan song" to designate a poet's last song before his death, when "they mercilessly kill it to hear its song." Since figurative painting is on its way out (this was written at the height of cubist art), it can no longer be used as a sign. "Sous le nom d'eider, les cygnes aidèrent à l'édredon" because the eider's feathers are used for stuffing quilts; it might be noted that the wordplay also suggests the name Leda and, by extension, refers to her encounter with Zeus disguised as a swan.

Finally, faithful to the encyclopedia, the poem makes a full circle by returning to the poet-swan and the "faux col" in the last sentence: the swan-men have long necks ("cous," whose popular etymology could be "col," repeating "faux col") like swans or like Fénelon (Féne-long, referring to the swan's long neck). They are also "insignes" symbolizing the nobility of literature and French culture, for Fénelon, "Cygne de Cambrai," is known for "la grâce et la pureté de son style" (*Larousse Encyclopédique*, 1960). We thus return to Mallarmé and to Baudelaire's exiled poet-swan.

7 ⬡

Diversions

Each magician's trick contains a number of telltale signs which expose it as an illusion. Certain arcane utterances, a dazzling way of gesticulating, the performer's costume and paraphernalia are all part of a network of indications which symbolically point to the fact that it is only a trick. Far from revealing the mechanics of the trick, however, these signs of illusion tend instead to conceal them: having learned that he is only dealing with an illusion, the spectator focuses his attention on the sleight of hand; he lets himself be captivated by the gimmickry in the hopes of learning "how it works," in order to explain rationally what he knows to be an illusion. But the more attention he pays to the processes, the less he understands them and the more mystified he becomes. In fact, the magician seems to depend on the spectator's "How does he do it?" to free his hands and prepare the next trick, to manipulate with greater ease and without the spectator's noticing it. One moment's trick serves as a diversion for the next, to the point that the magician who has mastered his act becomes completely hidden by it. In the eyes of the increasingly mystified spectator, the magician becomes a bona fide, supernaturally powerful sorcerer. It is only at the conclusion of the performance, when his practical skill is applauded, that the mask is allowed to fall.

In a number of respects, the mechanics of magic tricks present analogies with those of some poems from *Le Cornet à dés*. Although set in different contexts and involving different themes, both the trick and the poem, for example, follow the pattern of mystification-demystification which I have previously described. But it is especially in reference to the concept of intentionally diverting the reader's attention that this analogy is most illuminating, for one of Max Jacob's many definitions of art specifically states that "art is strictly speaking a *distraction*." He goes on to say: "I am not mistaken: this is the theory that has provided us with a marvelous race of heroes, with powerful evocations of milieus in which the legitimate curiosities and aspirations of the bourgeois, prisoners of themselves, are satisfied. But we must give the word 'distraction' a still broader significance. A work of art is a force that attracts, that absorbs the available strength of whoever approaches it" ("Préface de 1916," *1*; p. 21).

Very much like the magical illusion, or more specifically like the diversion of the mask-trick, the poem serves to distract the reader, to draw his attention to its texture and thereby free him from his earthly bonds, letting him believe that what he sees or reads is genuinely fantastical. Similarly the poet, masked by his bewildering prestidigitation, is freed and escapes; he too becomes momentarily and artificially superhuman. But here the mechanics of the poem diverge from those of the magic trick, with potentially dangerous consequences for the poet. If the magician is brought down to earth by the audience's applause, the poet, by the fact that he is not applauded at the poem's completion, runs the risk of remaining suspended in his illusory state. The cycle thus remains open: a dangerous malfunction that threatens to strand the poet in this state occurs in the mechanism of mystification-demystification; the poet runs the risk of becoming the mask, or at least doubting his own authenticity and believing in the possibility that he has actually been transformed into a magician or poet. It is at this moment that play borders on non-play, that exchanges between the reader and the poet are no longer possible.

Nuit infernale

Quelque chose d'horriblement froid tombe sur mes épaules. Quelque chose de gluant s'attache à mon cou. Une voix vient du ciel qui crie: "Monstre!" sans que je sache si c'est de moi et

de mes vices qu'il s'agit ou si l'on m'indique d'ailleurs l'être
visqueux qui s'attache à moi.

(*16*; p. 78)

At the opening of the text, the serenity of the night is disrupted and transformed into an infernal nightmare. This
fantasy consists of a play between a self and a "non-self,"
which is nevertheless a part of it, a "quelque chose," a shiver
provoked by external cold and yet also by internal fear. It
even appears that the very word "froid" functions as a vehicle
for the incessant movement between the self and the non-
self, a cold that is both physical (temperature) and psychological, as in the expression "shivers down the spine." In the
second sentence the physical phenomenon becomes even
more psychological. It is now quite near and sticky; and as it
approaches it takes on a mysterious and incomprehensible
character. This phenomenon roughly constitutes a manifes-
tation of the anguish felt by the mesmerized poet who cannot
divert his attention from the monster of uncertain origin
which grabs him by the neck and paralyzes him. Once this
"cold" monster has passed onto a psychological plane, it is
itself thought of as fantasy, a product of the imagination, in
other words as an artificial mask very much like the poem in
question. The monster and the poet, however, are in that
dangerous zone in which they risk losing their value as fiction
and becoming a disturbing reality. At the end of the text, the
poet is no longer able to identify the monster, to define it or
even to distinguish it from himself; he does not know who is
the monster: he with his *vices*, or the "*viscous* being," as
though the word "vice" was the factor which does not permit
the distinction.

The same process of blurring distinctions can be seen in
the following poem:

La Guerre

Les boulevards extérieurs, la nuit, sont pleins de neige; les
bandits sont des soldats; on m'attaque avec des rires et des
sabres, on me dépouille: je me sauve pour retomber dans un
autre carré. Est-ce une cour de caserne, ou celle d'une au-

berge? Que de sabres! que de lanciers! il neige! on me pique
avec une seringue: c'est un poison pour me tuer; une tête de
squelette voilée de crêpe me mord le doigt. De vagues
réverbères jettent sur la neige la lumière de ma mort.

(4; p. 29)

This text is one of the "prophetic" poems which Max Jacob
referred to at the beginning of the collection.[1] It is not, however, by considering it as historical prophecy that the poem
may be grasped; understanding lies instead within the play
aspect of the collection. At first the poet, no doubt at his window, is looking outside at the boulevards, a black and white
scene of night and snow. Suddenly, the setting is internalized
and becomes an agonizing, demoniac experience. The setting
becomes the scene of a battle in which the poet is attacked
from all sides. He becomes, in effect, a piece, perhaps the
bishop ("le fou"), on a chessboard, pursued by bandits of the
night turned soldiers. To save himself, the "fou" moves to
another square, then goes from square to square in a mad
dash, not knowing whether he has reached an enemy barracks (black) or a sanctuary, "une auberge" (white.) In this
bizarre game of chess, the piece in question does not know
itself, does not know whether it belongs to the whites or the
blacks, to good or to evil. Even the enemy is characterized by
the same ambiguity, as it too changes colors: from "il neige"
we move to "on me pique avec une seringue: c'est un poison
pour me tuer," and then to "une tête de mort," the white-on-
black emblem of poison and death. At each step the poet's
fear increases: the progression is from a "froid picotement"
to a "seringue" and finally to a skull which "bites" his finger,
just as the French speak of "manger" ("eating") pieces in
chess. The poem ends with an ambiguity similar to the one
described earlier in "Nuit infernale": a black and white image
appears at the window of the cornered poet, who is on the

---

1. See his "Avis," in *Le Cornet*: "Les poèmes qui font allusion à la guerre
ont été écrits vers 1909 et peuvent être dits prophétiques" (p. 26). (The
poems which contain allusions to war were written about 1909 and can be
called prophetic). My translation.

verge of being devoured: death on the snow and "la lumière
de ma mort" (black and white). He can no longer be distinguished from the enemy: the demon and death are part of
him; the laughter at the beginning of the poem would therefore be that of Baudelaire's Melmoth, who attacks both others
and himself.[2]

As in the preceding poem, the evil spirit in "Ruses du
démon pour ravoir sa proie" emanates from a mysterious setting, but this time it becomes attached to the poet after the
struggle:

> Le quai sombre, en triangle de donjon, hérissé de platanes
> l'hiver, squelettes trop jolis sur l'échancrure du ciel. A l'auberge
> vivait avec nous une femme belle, mais plate, qui cachait ses
> cheveux sous une perruque ou du satin noir. Un jour au-des-
> sus du granit, elle m'apparut au plein soleil de la mer: trop
> grande—comme les rochers du coin—elle mettait sa chemise,
> je vis que c'était un homme et je le dis. La nuit sur une espèce
> de quai londonien j'en fus châtié: éviter le coup de couteau à
> la face! se faire abîmer le pouce! riposter par un poignard
> dans la poitrine à la hauteur de l'omoplate. L'Hermaphrodite
> n'était pas mort. Au secours! au secours! on arrive . . . des
> hommes, que sais-je? ma mère! et je revois la chambre
> d'auberge sans serrure aux portes: il y avait, Dieu merci, des
> crochets mais quelle malignité a l'hermaphrodite: une ouver-
> ture du grenier, un volet blanc remue et l'hermaphrodite de-
> scend par là.
>
> (*47*; p. 219)

The external setting is a kind of cubist painting in which
geometrical shapes are blended and transformed and in
which the limits between the sky, the earth, and the sea are
blurred: the parallel lines of a quay take the form of a triangle, which evokes a macabre image: a dungeon "hérissé de
platanes" and no doubt also "hérissé," "bristling," with fear.
The ambiguity of the geometrical shapes continues with
"échancrure du ciel," also a kind of triangle, as the word

2. "De l'essence du rire," *Œuvres complètes* (1855; rpt. Paris: Seuil, 1968),
pp. 370–78).

"échancrure" is generally used to designate a coastal inlet or the neckline of a dress. This external setting suggests at the same time a certain consistency, not only through the presence of such distinct shapes as the quay, the triangle, and the skeleton, but also through the alliteration of the letter *r* in such words as "triangle," "hérissé," "échancrure." The first sentence thus becomes utterly ambiguous, evoking, on the one hand, a lack of distinction and, on the other, clearly delineated forms.

The second sentence introduces a setting characterized by slightly more security: an inn, unlike the dungeon on the outside. Yet it appears that the poet's imagination has carried some of the ambiguity into the inn, as it is inhabited by a woman as flat as the external "échancrure" (she is even compared to the "rochers du coin"), "quai," and "triangle." Furthermore, she hides her hair (and could thus be taken for a man) beneath a wig—yet another ambiguity. The ambiguities of the setting, evoked once again by "the sun of the sea," soon become completely incarnated in the body of this formerly lovely woman, who is now too big and hard, like the rocks and granite to which she is compared. The poet first transforms her into a man and informs her of that fact: this naturally arouses her anger and prompts her to seek revenge. The poet counters with a knife blow (the knife is yet another triangle) to the scapula, the "omoplate" (to be read as "homoplate"). He then transforms her into a hermaphrodite, a being as ambiguous as the setting, a monster, a chimera from his imagination, which pursues him into an inn, now no longer secure since the room has no lock and since "men" and his mother (the symbol of security) are unable to rescue him. The inn thus becomes as much a triangle as the dungeon—a fact confirmed by the final image in the poem: the poet cornered by the monster in the triangular attic.

"Poème du Java de M. René Ghil et s'appelant les Ksours" has the same electrifying quality, but here there are marks of a burlesque mechanism which indicate a falseness to the situation, and thus a greater degree of control exerted by the poet on this text than on the previous ones:

Avec un coup d'ongle, elles entrent le pli de leurs paupières
pour donner aux yeux le regard des statues. On n'a plus le
droit de dormir ici. Celles qui ont des yeux comme leurs cerfs
café au lait . . . Oh! ton diadème phallus de corail, Tao-Phen-
Tsu! . . . On ne les oubliera plus. Trois nains, officiers de ma-
rine, descendirent dans le précipice couleur champagne pour
faire la boulalaïka, avec des hétaïres de Champagne et, cette
nuit-là, deux élèves d'une école quittèrent leur . . . (ici quelque
égarement qui ne messied pas) pour jouer un duo de bigo-
phones peints sous les préaux de ces . . . électriques. Avec un
coup d'ongle, elles entrent le pli de leurs paupières pour donner à leurs yeux le regard des statues, mais celles qui ont des
yeux comme des vierges en sucre ne veulent jamais qu'on y
touche. On chante cette langue de cigale et les dieux-princes
mangent des tartines du bout des ongles.

(*15*; p. 77)

The poem opens with a mere "coup d'ongle," a nail scratch-
ing down the page, which involves the reader and the poet in
its hazardous magic. "Hazardous" because it initiates the
game of chance, draws the reader and the poet into the game
in spite of themselves by means of the first word written or
read, which commits them to carry their respective activities
through to the end. They become, in a sense, the "serfs" of
the poem's magic, just as the poet becomes the slave of the
cast dice; they are transfixed by the nightmare, they no
longer have "the right to sleep here," to forget the nightmare,
a scene they are all the more constrained to watch because
their eyes have the immobile "look of statues" and cannot be
shut. The magic becomes even more compelling when we
learn that it is imposed by the poem (or the dice or the "coup
d'ongle")—that is, comes from without, since the "coup
d'ongle" is not the poet's own. The result is a struggle between these factors external to the self and the will to be rid
of them, which reinforces the enchantment. In keeping with
its nature as mask, the poem as "coup d'ongle" also comes
from without: it is as if the poet had donned this magic mask
and found it impossible to remove it. The same is true for the
reader whose attention is so thoroughly riveted on the mask
that he is unable to demystify it and resituate the poet.

There is nevertheless evidence in the poem of a certain effort to exert control over the magic. Throughout these ostensibly enchanting lines we find a certain craftsmanship, a certain fiction which exposes them for what they are: human artifacts. Let us consider first of all the mystifying effects. The title, for example, seems to consist of nothing but a series of word associations designed to produce a cabalistic effect: "Java," "M. René Ghil" (a poet contemporary with Jacob, whose name has an exotic sound but whose poetry does not appear to be relevant to this poem, except that the theme here is that of poetic creation), and "les Ksours" (a mysterious-sounding African mountain range). Note also the following sentence: "Celles qui ont des yeux comme leurs cerfs café au lait." Despite the peculiar quality of this line, it is clear that the play on words "leur sert café au lait" represents a calculated effect that depreciates the magic by revealing that it is contrived. The poem contains other wordplays, such as "couleur champagne" and "hétaïres de Champagne," and "boulalaïka," a word fabricated from "balalaika," which (for the sake of decency) becomes a "bigophone" in connection with the schoolboys.

The words "Oh! ton diadème phallus de corail, Tao-Phen-Tsu!" also have an enchanting sonority, but "phallus de corail" provides an erotic counterpart to the image of the nail poked in the eye. This erotic element can be associated with the overall mesmerizing effect of the entire poem by virtue of the loss of control in the conscious subject during the erotic act. Erotic suggestions occur throughout the poem, intermingled with the entrancing elements already described: the three dwarfs, freakish beings, make "boulalaïka"—a word whose meaning is unclear but whose erotic connotations are unmistakable in context—with harlots. The schoolboys' activity also has erotic connotations, first because the poet is too modest to mention what they are doing, and second because they are playing the "bigophone," whose dimensions recall the "phallus de corail."

The mask can be recognized not only through the wordplays and the erotic innuendos, but also through the types of activity engaged in by these fantastical characters who all seem, in effect, to be performing a scene in a burlesque drama: dwarfs, which are often included in this type of drama, do the "boulalaïka" while the students play the "bigophone," a vulgar instrument made of cardboard (another mark of falseness), often seen on the burlesque stage. This "langue de cigale" finally undergoes a complete demystification in the last line, where prince-gods are eating bread and jam from the tips of their fingernails." We are simply dealing, then, with a child who is having an afternoon snack of "café au lait" with "sucre" and "tartines." The poem thus takes the form of a double diversion: the first serves to distract the reader, to engage him in a certain "electric" magic, to conceal the poet behind a magician's mask; and the second serves to distract a child, to entice him into eating his snack with a fantastic tale. The second diversion, however, provides the means of demystifying the first, and makes it possible for the poet, as well as the reader, momentarily to win the game.

In "Métempsychose" we again find a diversion based upon a seemingly magical and mystifying effect; but, in this case, the effort to gain control of the situation fails because the poet is taken in by the illusion:

> Ici ténèbres et silence! les mares de sang ont la forme des nuages. Les sept femmes de Barbe-Bleue ne sont plus dans le placard. D'elles il ne reste que cette cornette en organdi! Mais là-bas! là-bas! sur l'Océan, voilà sept galères, sept galères dont les cordages pendent des huniers dans la mer comme des nattes aux épaules des femmes. Elles approchent! elles approchent! elles sont là!
>
> (*42*; p. 179)

The poem begins by setting up a spatial-temporal context with the word "ici," which introduces the reader to a world of black magic. The poet seeks to conjure up a realm of "darkness and silence," a mystifying world in which the reader can find no reference points because the sky and the earth are indistinguishable: "the pools of blood" of Bluebeard's slain wives "are shaped like clouds," which are doubtless inflamed by a sunset, transformed by the poet into a macabre scene with a flourish of his sorcerer's wand. The reader has actually witnessed a prestidigitator's trick; he has watched the poet, disguised by a superhuman magician's mask, make Bluebeard's seven wives disappear from the cupboard in which they had been shut up. In their place he has left only a diaphanous "cornette en organdi" (organdy coif) through which the contents might have escaped. But, this being a poem about metempsychosis, the souls of the women escape, only to become incarnated in the galleys and thus imprisoned in another object. This transference from object to object explains the unusual spelling of "métempsy-chose," which does not have an *h* in French and which denotes the transference of objects, "chose(s)." The poet's trick has backfired, however, for the souls appear to be triumphing over their new physical form: the galleys have ropes like braids; they are victorious over the imprisoning object. The power of the galley-wives has become so great that they turn the tables and take the offensive against the terrified poet, bewildered by the fact that his own magic now moves relentlessly toward him, threatening, so it seems, to absorb him.

"L'Âme de la Joconde" also deals with metempsychosis, but here it is treated with irony and is therefore much more under control:

> Le Jocond! c'est le réveille-matin de la baronne! Il a l'âme de la Joconde, il s'arrête ou marche au gré des aventures de ce malheureux tableau. La police aurait pu le consulter, jadis, il aurait répondu comme certaines tables à leurs fidèles. Cette pièce d'horlogerie vient de Florence ou de la Forêt-Noire: elle habite une colonnade en acajou et cuivre et ne quitte pas la voyageuse baronne. Elle sonne, la belle s'éveille et pense. On dit que l'âme de la Joconde inspire à la baronne ses beaux poèmes et ses tableaux et que le grand ressort se brisera à jamais quand elle s'avisera de prendre un nouvel amant. Le Jocond n'a pas besoin d'être remonté pour aller son tran-tran de pendule; toutefois, la femme de chambre aide en cachette à la féerie. Personne n'aide à la féerie de là baronne, sinon la Jo-

conde elle-même, dont le sourire mystérieux veille la nuit à son chevet.

(38; p. 132)

To the naïve reader, the title of this poem indicates a sentimental reverie based on the famous portrait whose smile is so "realistic" that it is said to be alive. Yet even the title contains a measure of irony, for it appears that Max Jacob has exaggerated the conceptual cliché about the painting's vitality by giving it a soul. The interruption of the reader's reverie is completed by the first words of the poem: "Le Jocond" is defeminized, depoeticized; it acts like an "alarm clock," effacing the portrait's enigmatic smile and jolting the reader out of his reverie. These words set in motion a certain mechanical enchantment in which expectations and paradigms of ownership are set up only to be immediately destroyed: the "Jocond" has "La Joconde's" soul (his wife's or the portrait's), as does Bluebeard in "Métempsychose." The soul is so attached to him that it becomes his mistress and he, who is its owner, becomes its slave: "il s'arrête ou marche au gré des aventures de ce malheureux tableau" and can inform the police of its whereabouts (at the time the poem was written, the painting had been stolen). A degree of ambiguity nevertheless persists, permitting the naïve reader's reverie to continue; it can be said that La Joconde is so much in love with her husband, Le Jocond, that he "possesses her soul." In fact, a certain amorous intrigue develops between La Joconde and the baroness, who, it seems, is so much in love with the portrait's smile that she is willing to accept a substitute, a false representation: a Florentine alarm clock which, like Le Jocond, encloses La Joconde's soul.

This Jocond/Joconde/alarm clock continues its romance with its new mistress (in the sense of both lover and owner): it inspires the baroness to paint and to compose poems and, if she were ever to leave it, its heart (mainspring) would be broken. Their love, however, is far from perfect because the alarm clock is not wound up, meaning that its heart or

mainspring has not been recharged with love by the baroness, "la femme de chambre aide en cachette à la féerie," as is
often the case with fictional amorous entanglements. This
poem might even be read as a parody of a tale by La Fontaine
titled "Le Joconde," in which a hero of that name leaves home
to perform amorous exploits, only to realize along the way
that he has forgotten the portrait which his wife urged him
to take along as a souvenir. Returning to his castle at night,
he finds his wife in bed with an ugly servant. Max Jacob has
transformed the wife in the tale into Le Jocond, who in the
poem is unfaithful to his mistress, the baroness. She, however, feels no need to repay her lover in kind, as in La Fontaine's tale—that is, to become unfaithful and seek affairs out
of vengeance—for she satisfies her erotic needs with the help
of the portrait's mysterious smile whose soul transcends the
matter of the painting. In other words, "personne n'aide à la
féerie de la baronne" because she creates her own fantasies
and romance by imagining that the alarm clock is the authentic smiling portrait.

The baroness's enchantment is like that of the poet writing
the poem (like the poet, the baroness is even inspired by the
painting to write pretty poems): both construct a spurious
fantasy, the baroness with the help of an alarm clock, the poet
with the help of a mask, and both mystify the reader and
leave him with an ironic smile which asserts the superiority of
their deceit. With the help of this lingering smile, the poem
becomes circular, returning to the portrait in the title, which
had induced the reader's sentimental reverie. Yet the smile is
not directed solely at the reader, but also at the poem and its
content: her smile could also be a measure of mockery in La
Joconde's attitude toward the baroness, who was taken in by
Le Jocond as alarm clock. She thus demystifies the poem's
enchantment in much the same way as the reader tried to
demystify the poem, with a smile . . . .

8 ⬡

Translations

Le réel ne prend corps, forme et
sens que sous forme de message
qu'interprète un observateur/con-
cepteur. Nous n'avons de la
réalité que des traductions,
jamais la V.O.
—Edgar Morin, *La Méthode I, La nature de la nature*

In this chapter I would like to approach the concept
of play in Max Jacob's writing from a perspective different
from those presented in earlier chapters. It may therefore be
useful to reiterate what has been discovered thus far. I noted
a certain barrier to communication in Max Jacob. The figure
of the *obstacle* was adopted to discuss that barrier: a term sufficiently generalized and unlocalized to convey the ability for
the barrier to assume a virtually unlimited number of forms.
What mattered most about the obstacle was that it be maintained. Although there were never any actual transgressions
of this obstacle, there were pseudo-transgressions, which I
chose to designate as *masks*: Max Jacob needed to project a
fictional identity in order to write, but this identity never con-
cealed another one.

In the chapters titled "Riddles," "Parodies," and "Diversions," a number of poems from *Le Cornet à dés* were grouped
into three categories of masks. I found that communication,
the obstacle to communication, and the pseudo-transgression
of that obstacle were all caught up in a more or less definable
network: each mask, that is to say each poem, had a mystify-

ing function which permitted the poet to move toward another position; and the reader, by the very act of reading, was
ensnared by this staging. This reading had a dual value, however, in that it also served to demystify the text. Demystification did not consist of determining what lay behind the mask:
there was no solution of the riddle, no identification of the
text parodied, no identification of that from which attention
was being diverted. There was instead a discovery and an ap-
preciation of the mask *as mask*, as an object to be seen and
felt. This material apprehension of the mask had the effect,
not of conveying the mystified and mystifying poet back to
some original subjectivity, neither known nor articulated, but
rather of reducing the poem to that zero degree where nothing remained: the void that permitted a new beginning, the
fabrication of another mask, another poem.

Up to this point in the discussion, I have dealt only in general terms with a notion that is perhaps more fundamental
than any other to Max Jacob's poetry. This is the notion of
communication—a notion that is of particular importance in-
sofar as it concerns the problems of translation and representation. I now propose to examine this notion in detail; and, in
so doing, I hope to amplify—not contradict—some of my
earlier claims.

The *ideal* translation entails the complete transfer of meaning from one form to another. Notwithstanding the expenditure of energy invested in this transfer, there is, again ideally,
no loss of information. As in the case of representation, a
substance is given a new form, a new skin. The ideal translation thus resembles taxidermy: it is the domain of the repetition of the same, the realm of redundance—the essential
condition for a passage of information. It is also the domain
of paraphrase, of interpretation, and of fidelity. Yet for there
to be a transfer of meaning, the intermediary or medium
must be neutral, insignificant, self-effacing; he must assume
the role of the postman who brings news without knowing
what he carries, who continues his rounds after delivering
the message. He must be like a telegraph wire or even like

paper: he must neither think about nor act upon the information he transports; he must not mutilate and, ideally, he must not transform the message. Everything passes, both good and bad, and this can occur only because the transmitters "work" as automatons, transporting a message while unaware of its content. In other words, for the transmitters to function normally and efficiently, the theory that engendered them must contain an "independence" clause, must postulate a separation between container and contained, between the envelope and the letter, the transmitter and the message, the representer and the represented. This clause is the cornerstone of the ideal translation.

Let us imagine, however, a different situation, one in which the postman was called upon to read the letters he carried, and, in consequence, was subjected to the information therein and, possibly, acted upon it. This situation would extend indefinitely, if not ultimately arrest, the circulation of information: the postman would now sort the mail on the basis of content and no longer on the basis of the envelope—which is always a lateral procedure. The postman's interference—the noise of transmission—would be louder than the information itself; the postman's voice alone would be heard; he would become a "parasite" that obliterated the letter. A postman cognizant of the content of the information he carried would, in effect, constitute the ideal disruption of this information. Likewise, the translator—the real, not an ideal, one—who must read and understand the material in order to give it a new form and transmit it, disrupts the message. He institutes noise or, better yet, *is* noise, and thus transforms the message. Any transfer to a new form necessarily entails transformation. Pushed to an extreme, the result of translation is what could be termed the *untranslated*: something which derives from a primary text (an event, "nature," or even thought or "imagination"), yet which does not transmit that text, something which makes an appeal to the text yet differs completely from it, something which claims to be representative, imitative, yet neither represents nor imitates, something which seeks identity yet achieves difference. If, in other words, the function of ordinary communication is to "reach maximum entropy as swiftly as possible,"[1] translation disrupts such perfect imitation by deforming it. Certain forms nonetheless resist the translator's noise: the words of the target-language create a resonance that evokes the signified of the source-language. The result is "a new form, dislocated into locally stable elements,"[2] that act as a *memory* of the primary text, of that which has been conveyed, translated.

In Max Jacob's poetry these forms tend to lose some of their local and relative stability. I have considered the example of opposing images in "galop élastique dans la verdure" *or* "les poussiéreux bas-reliefs" (see Chapter 2). This is not an isolated example in *Le Cornet à dés*. The word "or," mark of the alternative, frequently occurs in these texts. Most often this alternative serves as an index of the undecidability of the source-text and consequently of its loss. Let us read the beginning of "Conte de Noël":

> Il y avait une fois un architecte ou un cheval: c'était un cheval plutôt qu'un architecte, à Philadelphie, à qui on avait dit: "Connais-tu la cathédrale de Cologne? fais construire une cathédrale pareille à la cathédrale de Cologne!"
>
> (*18*; p. 81)

Following his initial indecision, the poet opts for the horse, yet continues to speak as though he were referring to an architect. This is therefore not about an architect-horse or a horse-architect in some surrealistic fantasy; in other words, one cannot read this text as if it were about a horse, yet persist in seeing some connoted architect (or the opposite; it does not matter). This is not an ambiguous text; the ambiguity resides solely in the perception at the beginning of the poem. The text can only be decoded in a single direction, in favor

---

1. René Thom, *Modèles mathématiques de la morphogenèse* (Paris: Union Générale d'Éditions, 1974), p. 215.
2. Ibid., p. 234.

of the architect, but this reading emerges after the designation of a mooring point, subsequently destroyed.

The title plays the same role with regard to the text: an anchoring followed by an uprooting. The telling of fairy tales depends upon the familiarity of the reader or listener who knows all the fairy tales, especially those about Christmas, for whom all such tellings are always retellings, and who will listen to this one for the sheer pleasure of hearing it repeated. "Once upon a time there was" announces, among other things, that "I am going to tell you a story that you surely know"; the listener, like an attentive computer, will try to recognize the tale that is being *repeated* for his enjoyment. In Max Jacob's text, however, this frame of reference explodes as soon as I read "once upon a time there was *an architect*"; even if there were such a tale about an architect, or if I pretended there was one in order to conceal my ignorance or to avoid spoiling the narration, I would lose my second (fictitious) reference point as soon as I read " . . . or a horse." Reference becomes impossible; the message also announces the lack of a message: the postman admits he is inventing the letters he delivers; what has been conveyed becomes the untranslated. But the rest of the poem is precisely about art— art that does not pass from one locality to another, from one space to another:

> Et, comme il ne connaissait pas la cathédrale de Cologne, alors, il fut mis en prison. Mais, en prison, un ange lui apparut, qui lui dit: "Wolfrang! Wolfrang! pourquoi te désoles-tu? — Il me faut rester en prison, parce que je ne connais pas la cathédrale de Cologne! — Il te manque le vin du Rhin pour bâtir la cathédrale de Cologne, mais fais-leur voir le plan, alors tu pourras sortir de prison." Et l'ange lui donna le plan, et il montra le plan, alors il put sortir de prison, mais jamais il ne put bâtir la cathédrale, parce qu'il ne trouvait pas le vin du Rhin. Il eut l'idée de faire venir du vin du Rhin à Philadelphie, mais on lui envoya un affreux vin français de la Moselle, de sorte qu'il ne put bâtir la cathédrale de Cologne à Philadelphie; il ne fit qu'un affreux temple protestant.

Just as the poet could not re-call the source-text (horse or architect), the architect cannot construct the cathedral of Cologne in Philadelphia; he cannot convey, trans-late, it to another space. The reason for this failure, as I shall attempt to demonstrate, is also a matter of repetition—not the repetition of meaning in different forms, as in translation; but, because we are dealing with artistic *forms* (a cathedral), the repetition of forms, of signifiers. Let us take the expression "cathédrale de Cologne," which is repeated no less than six times throughout the text (and twice more for the word "cathédrale" alone). This repetition serves to draw attention not only to the meaning of the expression but also to its actual form. Here there is another repetition, that of the [k] sound in the two principal morphemes of expression, as though this sound were the cornerstone of the cathedral. Once we have noted this repetition, others emerge: first, *vin du Rhin* (an expression that also occurs three times in the text) which, as we are told, is needed to build/convey/translate the cathedral of Cologne to Philadelphia. It is as if a pair of repetitious connectors were indispensable to this process. It is as if a pair of [ɛ̃] sounds were needed to carry out a project (transporting from one place to another) that involved another pair of sounds [k].

There is another necessity involved in conveying the "vin du Rhin" to Philadelphia, a necessity which links this project to other themes discovered earlier to be operating in *Le Cornet à dés*. The "vin du Rhin" comes from the same space as the object to be imitated. It will enable the imitator to be conveyed, translated—imaginatively, of course—back to the source while remaining in his target-space; it will permit his "experiencing" the source, the begetter of the cathedral; it will enable him to understand it perfectly in order to reproduce it perfectly. But upon closer consideration this architect—he whose principal function is usually to produce the original text, the archi-text—is asked to produce, not an original, but a copy; he does not know the cathedral and is locked up. Here we come upon a theme widespread in the collection: that of the imprisoned poet who cannot copy the coveted object. The theme, however, has been inverted in this instance: he is imprisoned *because* he cannot execute a copy. After he is imprisoned, the secret of the original is whispered to him, thereby reducing even further his function of architect.

It is the repetition of signifiers, however, that provides the greatest insight into the logic of this text. The repetition of [ɛ̃] and [k] permits resolving the initial undecidability between "cheval" and "architecte." What accounts for the confusion is not what the words represent but rather the words themselves: the fact that both contain the sound [ʃ]. It is also clear why Max Jacob opted for "cheval" over "architecte": this so-called architect simply transports items from one place to another, like a horse. Thus, if the poet declares that "it" is a horse yet continues to discuss "it" as if "it" were an architect, it is because he ultimately demonstrates that "it" conducts itself like a horse: a means of transporting pure and simple forms. The resolution of the poem is now clear: unable to obtain "*vin* du Rh*in*" for his "*cathédrale de Cologne*," he gets, or rather is sent, "un *affreux* vin *fr*ançais de la Moselle." And what could be the result of linking this pair of connectors with the plan whispered by the angel, if not "un *affreux* temple *p*rotestant"; the sounds of "fr" in "a*ffr*eux" and "*fr*ançais" necessarily infect the result to the point of reproduction: the repetition of an entire word (affreux) in the result. But what of this poor architect? Wasn't he destined to fail from the beginning, from his origin, ever since his "archi-" (origin)? For his name is not Wolfgang, as one might have supposed from a hasty reading, but rather Wol*fr*ang, in which we find that awful "fr" sound inscribed since his birth (it is tempting to ask whether, with such a name, he could have built anything else!). Yet not only is the "fr" inscribed in his name, so too is the "fran" of the "vin *fr*ançais." It is therefore not surprising that he received a "vin *fr*ançais" instead of a "vin du Rhin," and that he builds an "a*ffr*eux *tem*ple *pro*testant" suffused with *fran*cophonic redundancies.

Wolfrang invites further consideration from the standpoint of ideal versus real translation. Whereas the task of the ideal translator is to repeat a meaning in a different form, Wolfrang must repeat the same form in another space. In one respect, Wolfrang is completely faithful to the transmission, not of the message, but of the form: he brings back only what he has received laterally—the plan of the cathedral, the morphemes which he has inherited with his name and those which necessarily accompanied the wine he was sent. In respect, however, to his initial project—that is, repeating the cathedral—these inherited forms function as "subjective" interference precisely because he utilizes them in a dumb and lateral fashion, like an automaton. The project is thus disrupted by "subjective" forms which transform it into an entirely new entity retaining nevertheless a "memory" of the original. And one could say that this transformation is the direct result of a faithful (objective, automatic) use of inherited forms. Here we find yet another instance of a previously discussed theme, that of the interference of the internal, of the self, in the apprehension of the external (see Chapter 4). Furthermore, the presence in this text of a project of imitation, its disruption, and a transformation of the imitated object—in other words, a loss of foundation for which is substituted a logic of the surface—associates this text with the notion of play as I described it in general (Chapter 2) and as I described it specifically with regard to Max Jacob (Chapters 3 and 4). The notion of translation, as a matter of fact, will serve Max Jacob as a privileged tool for subverting reference, foundation, and meaning.

Poème

"Que veux-tu de moi, dit Mercure.
—Ton sourire et tes dents, dit Vénus.
—Elles sont fausses. Que veux-tu de moi?
—Ton caducée.
—Je ne m'en sépare point.
—Viens l'apporter ici, divin facteur."

Il faut lire cela dans le texte grec: cela s'appelle *Idylle*. Au collège, un ami, souvent refusé aux examens, me dit: "Si on traduisait en grec un roman de Daudet, on serait assez fort après pour l'examen! mais je ne peux pas travailler la nuit. Ça

fait pleurer ma mère!" Il faut lire aussi cela dans le texte grec,
messieurs; c'est une idylle, εἰδυλλοζ, petit tableau.

(*8*; p. 43)

This poem must, in fact, be read in the original Greek. It
must be read as something which has not been translated, or
as something whose translation is the process of a transformation, a disruption of the original. In French, "idylle" is a
small tableau or poem dealing with a rural or pastoral subject. In Greek, εἰδυλλοζ is also a "small form"; but, contrary to
the French, and through its association with εἰδωλον it is a
"form without substance," which no theme, rural or pastoral,
supports. εἰδωλον is a mirror image, just as the two parts of
this poem reflect one another, apply to one another, and can
be understood in terms of one another. It is nothing but a
film, a surface, a disembodied specter. Without being translated into French, that is, into the meaning it is given in
French, it is a form that leads nothing nowhere ("traduire"
comes from trans-ducere, to carry beyond), or else εἰδυλλοζ is
a translation which has lost what it carries (body, substance)
and fails to transmit it. Noise upstages the message; it is a
mask concealing nothing, a false skin representing nothing
but itself.

Mercury must also be read in reference to the Greek text:
he is Hermes, god of the circulation of goods, who dispels
phantoms and ghosts; he is god of messengers, of merchants,
and of communication, a patron of the arts and the inventor
of the lyre, and was originally a pastoral divinity as well. In
Max Jacob's text he clings to his smile, his teeth (which are
false), and to his scepter. He is therefore the exact opposite
of the Greek god—he inhibits circulation, commerce, and
communication; he is the postman who fails to transmit his
message (in spite of Venus's charm) since his smile, teeth, and
scepter remain with him. Moreover, instead of dispelling
phantoms and ghosts, he virtually cultivates them: his message is false, and he keeps it to himself. What Mercury actually bears are but the external signs of his function, the attributes which make him a postman (in particular his scepter).

In a sense, Venus asks the impossible of him: not to transmit a message, but to give her that which permits Mercury to transmit messages, the channel of communication. To surrender it would be to cancel himself out. This is perhaps his fault: instead of a message, he bears only the means of transmission, the grounds for the transfer— in other words, nothing but noise, an "idylle," a pure form: false teeth.

In similar fashion, Max Jacob's text, if it aspires to be a translation (transport an old story into a new space), folds back upon itself. The second part is not a transposition of the first, but its reflection. There is clearly a correlation between certain elements: for example, Hermes the messenger becomes a translator in the second part. Yet the correlation is inverted: the first part translates from Greek into French, and the second from French into Greek, while the word "idylle" appears in French within the Greek context, and in Greek within the French part. This is not a repetition of a fixed scheme, but its inverse reflection. The second is a false image—idyllic in the Greek sense—of the first: its mere phantom. Or vice versa. In both instances, communication is not carried out. Just as Mercury failed to release anything, the translator fails at translation. Once again, this failure stems from a "subjective" interference with the translation. The translator's problem, like Wolfrang's, is tied to his origins: he cannot work at night because it makes his mother cry. And night is the time for phantoms and ghosts, a time utterly inappropriate for *faithful* translations.

Phantoms and translations are thus linked in Max Jacob's poetry, and translations could aptly be described as ghosts: false, immaterial images which function only as memories of a primary form, the living being or the primary text. Yet for the primary text to produce such an immaterial reflection, there has to have been a "fault" in the perception (apprehension and comprehension) of the object—I am tempted to say a "fault" in the geological sense, a fissure, a flaw. In the poem just discussed, the fault resides in the disparity between two meanings of the word "idylle"; in "Conte de Noël," it was the problem of the alternative. But what of a text in which the choice is not simple (a choice between two entities—horse or architect, idylle or εἰδυλλοζ), but complex? Would this not constitute a more drastic subversion of the source-object, and would this process of negation not yield an even more acute understanding of communication and translation? Would it not provide insight into the true nature of Hermes?

> Traduit de l'allemand ou du bosniaque
> Mon cheval s'arrête! Arrête aussi le tien, compagnon, j'ai peur! entre les pentes de la colline et nous, les pentes gazonnées de la colline, c'est une femme, si ce n'est pas un grand nuage. Arrête! elle m'appelle! elle m'appelle et je vois son sein qui bat! son bras me fait signe de la suivre, son bras . . . si son bras n'est pas un nuage.
> — Arrête, compagnon, j'ai peur, arrête! entre les arbres de la colline, les arbres inclinés de la colline, j'ai vu un œil, si cet œil n'est pas un nuage. Il me fixe, il m'inquiète; arrête! Il suit nos pas sur la route, si cet œil n'est pas un nuage.
> — Écoute, compagnon! Fantômes, vies de cette terre ou d'une autre, ne parlons pas de ces êtres à la ville pour n'être pas traités d'importuns.
>
> (*19*; p. 82)

The title resembles an oxymoron: it makes a statement yet contains the negation of that very statement; it announces a translation yet casts doubt on translation. We are offered a text translated from the German *or* from the Bosnian; yet for it to be a translation, it would seem that its source would have to be stable—which is evidently not the case here: unsure of its origin, it claims nevertheless to be translated. It is a text whose source-text exists only as a memory, much like the mask masking nothing. It is a text which, so to speak, translates the untranslated, represses and obliterates its source. While it may resist the designation "translation," it nevertheless identifies itself as such, as the transfer of meaning from one place to another, but always intrinsically undermined. The title, which conventionally serves to translate, summarize, represent or announce the content, marks a break with the text which follows: to all appearances, the text is not a translation—neither from the German nor the Bosnian. The only relations between the text and title are of a formal nature: the title presides over the text, introduces the notion of alternatives which will recur in the text, and indicates the transfer of meaning which, in the text, will take the term of understanding and reporting to the city what has been seen.

The text tells the story of a vision, but the vision is ambiguous at several levels. In the first place, there is a concerted effort on the part of the subjects to repress the very fact that it is a vision. Following each apparition, the narrator promptly notes that what he has seen might have been a cloud, thereby neutralizing the vision by integrating it to the real. Furthermore, the apparition itself is ambiguous: is it a woman, her breast, her arm, or her eye? The ambiguity is even carried to a second degree: not only is there an ambiguity internal to this vision, a question of appearance versus reality, there is also the broader question of ambiguity versus univocality, translated versus untranslated. A closer consideration of the ambiguity of the vision (namely, the impossibility to decide among a woman, a breast, an arm, or an eye) reveals a certain directionality in which the reader (or the poet) moves from the general to the particular, from an overview to scrutiny of details.

Paralleling this quasi-vectorial movement is another on a topographical plane. In the first paragraph, a certain direction is indicated by the slopes of the hill, grassy slopes which facilitate a flow in a single direction. In the second paragraph, trees, leaning presumably in the same direction, grow on these same slopes. It is as if a perspective organized these elements, causing them all to converge on a fixed point: the eye pursuing the poet. Caught in this perspective, transported by the flow and the converging elements, it is as if we were being swept, against our will, toward this fixed point, toward the depth or the *meaning* of things. If translation conveys meaning, we appear to be carried toward it in this instance.

The translation, however, is called into question by an inverse movement, which is neither organized as were the converging elements, nor characterized by metamorphosis as

were the parts of the body. Instead, this movement is formed
solely by the repetition of an unvarying phrase: "if it isn't a
cloud." This phrase may be understood in different ways, yet
each functions as a negation: "unless it isn't a cloud and what
I see is actually an apparition"; or even "I hope it is a cloud."
In any event, the phrase plays the same role as the *or* of the
title and the *or* of the architect/horse: it serves to undermine
the vision and, thereby, the very schema of the direction. This
structure of alternative deprives the vision of a foundation
and transforms it into something that has neither body
(breast, arm . . .) nor substance. Nor does it have a source,
since it has several multiform sources; it is truly a cloud that
can neither be translated nor conveyed.

In the third paragraph the narrator in effect refers to the
vision as a phantom and, again, resorts to an alternative: "life
from this earth or from another." As a phantom without a
source, it is therefore not something to be reported back to
the city. Sourceless, directionless, and hence senseless, this
thing is untranslatable; to speak of it in town would surely be
to act as "importuns." This word can also be read in several
ways. Etymologically, it derives from "in" and "portus," that
is, without a; in other words, without origin or destina-
tion, between two ports, two locations, two categories of
being: "this life *or* another," "German *or* Bosnian." The
whimsy could be carried even further: "in portus" (which
does not carry) would signify "that which does not transport
or report" (the opposite of translation); that is, without ter-
restrial ties, unanchored, pure surface, play.

The preceding poem explains Max Jacob's fascination with
Fantomas, the subject of the following poem. Not only did
Max Jacob find in the name Fantomas a resonance of his own
preoccupations, but he also found sympathetic the fact that
the popular character was noted for his ability to generate
new forms for himself, new masks to suit new occasions. His
extraordinary adaptability and his virtual lack of memory (in
the strict sense of the term in that he never reverts to an original shape) provide him with the flexibility to shed all intrinsic
qualities: he can say, signify, represent, and be represented by

anything. In this sense he is the empty slot, the non-sense which says nothing because it says everything. He is also the untranslated because he translates everything; his translations are thus, in a sense, himself; he is what he translates. This is the highest degree of non-sense:[3] he is a spontaneous auto-translation, since he is the source-text, the target-text, and the channel of communication.

> Fantomas
> Sur le marteau de la porte en argent bruni, sali par le temps, sali par la poussière du temps, une espèce de Bouddha ciselé au front trop haut, aux oreilles pendantes, aux allures de marin ou de gorille: c'était Fantomas. Il tirait sur deux cordes pour faire venir là-haut je ne sais quoi. Son pied glisse; la vie en dépend; il faut atteindre la pomme d'appel, la pomme en caoutchouc avant le rat qui va la trouer. Or, tout cela n'est que de l'argent ciselé pour un marteau do porte.
>
> (*28*; p. 98)

In Max Jacob's text, there is no original Fantomas to be distinguished from his doubles. He appears only in disguise, yet this disguise in no way implies the existence of some un-disguised individual. In fact, in this text a search behind the mask would reveal only the doorknocker, as if the knocker existed first and Fantomas, as a true phantom, momentarily inhabited it. Fantomas never manifests himself, or rather can only manifest himself in disguise: he has no other existence. He is no more than his name: Fantomas, Idylle. It is interesting to compare Max Jacob's Fantomas to one of his recent avatars: Superman, for example, who spends his off-hours as a bespectacled, grey-suited journalist. In the case of Max Jacob's Fantomas, however, there is no alter ego: ask who he really is and you literally find nothing. Furthermore, Superman's disguise is itself a uni-form, whereas Fantomas is multi-form: in this text alone he appears as Buddha, gorilla, sailor, etc. If the journalist plays the role of Superman, Fantomas

---

3. For a development of the concept of non-sense, see Gilles Deleuze, *Logique du sens* (Paris: Minuit, 1969), pp. 83–91.

plays the role of Fantomas; this amounts to saying that, if a journalist lies behind the identity of Superman, Fantomas again lies behind all the figures of Fantomas. In this sense, Superman is a classical hero for whom the distinction between being and appearance is constant, whereas Max Jacob's Fantomas is a modern hero: a pure, self-generating form, undetermined by any content whatsoever.

Each language provides a grammatical means for distinguishing subject from predicate; from this distinction derives the possibility of identifying a topic and of recognizing commentary upon it. This principle is precisely what permits translation from one language to another: an equivalent topic is selected in the target-language, and an attempt is made to duplicate the commentary upon it. In the case of Fantomas, every effort to delineate him as a topic fails, just as the effort to establish the source of the vision in "Traduit de l'allemand ou du bosniaque" also failed. Without a topic, there evidently can be neither commentary nor translation. For Jacob's Fantomas there is, nevertheless, a commentary, a commentary, so to speak, without a topic, a true surface marked by the signifier: a story with certain suspenseful acrobatics: "faire venir de là-haut je ne sais quoi. Son pied glisse; la vie en dépend; il faut atteindre la pomme d'appel, la pomme en caoutchouc avant le rat qui va la trouer." The "pomme d'appel," the apple of appeal or the apple of apple, is a tautology worthy of Fantomas, who deprives subject and predicate, topic and commentary, of their value. "Or, tout cela n'est que de l'argent ciselé pour un marteau de porte." The phantom/Fantomas, pure film, will have disappeared after having borrowed a body, having undergone repeated metamorphosis and kept us in suspense for a spell.

I have discussed the interrelation between surface effects and an insistence upon the signifier in Max Jacob's poetry (see in particular Chapter 5 and the analysis of "Conte de Noël" in this chapter). The Fantomas poem provided yet another example of this association: invoking the name of Fantomas and insisting upon the signifier appear to have presupposed one another for Max Jacob. In the following poem, "Encore Fantomas," an obvious play on words, taken literally, acts as an organizing principle:

Encore Fantomas

Ils étaient aussi gourmets que gourmés, le monsieur et la dame. La première fois que le chef des cuisines vint, un bonnet à la main, leur dire: "Excusez-moi, est-ce que Monsieur et Madame sont contents?" on lui répondit: "Nous vous le ferons savoir par le maître d'hôtel!" La seconde fois, ils ne répondirent pas. La troisième fois, ils songèrent à le mettre dehors, mais ils ne purent s'y résoudre, car c'était un chef unique. La quatrième fois (mon Dieu, ils habitaient aux portes de Paris, ils étaient seuls toujours, ils s'ennuyaient tant!), la quatrième fois, ils commencèrent: "La sauce aux câpres est épatante, mais le canapé de la perdrix était un peu dur." On en arriva à parler sport, politique, religion. C'est ce que voulait le chef des cuisines, qui n'était autre que Fantomas.

(29; p. 99)

The difference between "gourmets" and gourmés" is of a graphemic order (one unpronounced letter, *t*, differentiates them) and therefore calls forth a reading of the surface and of the skin. The couple in the poem are "gourmets" but they are also "gourmés," that is to say, snobbish, stuffy, in that they will not deal directly with the cook. But the fact that they ultimately do confront the cook indicates similarities between their behavior and that of Fantomas: it appears that they wanted to speak with him all along, but, as Fantomas would have done, they conceal that desire by affecting airs. The resemblance to Fantomas is reinforced by the fact that they seem to have adopted this particular behavior on the basis of a homonymy: being "gourmets," they preferred to be "gourmés," as if their behavior could be regulated by the addition or deletion of a single letter. In other words, if Fantomas "inhabits" forms at will, the couple also "inhabits" forms that could be reduced to two nearly identical words, two words that sum them up and represent them, two words that function, in effect, as their *proper names*. Like Wolfrang, this couple is caught up in an onomastic network. For them, however, the network functions in a manner chronologically inverse to that of Wolfrang: first we are given their "names" (gourmets/gourmés), then we learn how they came to earn them; whereas, in the case of Wolfrang, we are given his story and only then realize that, *given his name*, that story could not have been otherwise.

Thus, for the couple, as well as for Wolfrang and Fantomas, the names explain the story—whatever it may be. It must be borne in mind, however, that these characters appear as they are as a result of having participated in a process of translation which malfunctioned, which failed to transform either part or all of something that was in the original version: for Wolfrang, it was the *fran* contained in his name; for Fantomas the question is moot because, being essentially proteiform, his infinite elasticity—his entirely metamorphosed and metamorphosing character—persists. For the couple, however, it appears at first that the translation lacks nothing in that it states precisely their names. But this is not the case. Translation marks the passage of meaning from one form to another. In "Encore Fantomas" the point of departure is not meaning, but a form—a play on words. This form is given a meaning which is placed in a context, on the basis of which a story is invented and constructed. In other words, this poem completely inverts the "normal" process of translation. "Gourmets" and "gourmés" are as worthy of the designation "untranslated" as is Wolfrang's *fran*. The importance of this phenomenon in Max Jacob's poetry cannot be overstated: translation falters because something from the original remains, because something remains untranslated.

The untranslated need not necessarily be a letter. The letter is merely its most concrete minimal representation. The untranslated may be any element intended to be processed or transformed by a code, but to which that code fails to apply. If one were to imagine, for example, a book—which by definition conveys something from another place or another time (either real or imaginary)—a book in which what is "conveyed" is exactly what is taking place at the moment at which it is being presented, then we would have "Fêtons la mort"

(*20*; p. 83), whose very simultaneity renders it untranslated. Or if one imagined a stage upon which some action was to be presented, yet upon which there appeared a player who does not act but who *is* himself, then we would have the "Soldat de Marathon" (*36*; p. 116). In both cases there is, in the midst of a complex circuit, a negation of representation which dictates to the book and to the player that they are representations. The negation of representation constitutes precisely what I have endeavored to describe as the untranslated. In concluding this chapter, I shall examine these two poems in the hope of reaching some conclusion about Max Jacob, if not about his name.

> Fêtons la mort
>
> "Je vais vous donner des places gratuitement! c'est deux francs cinquante!" Il s'agit d'une fête au Trocadéro pour se réjouir de la mort d'un célèbre écrivain russe qui entre dans la gloire. On distribue des livrets dont l'un est en bois sculpté d'une manière enfantine et l'autre illustré de couleurs. La mort du Russe est figurée par une blouse mauve foudroyée, tandis que Maroussia et Anna se penchent sur lui en grand costume national: nattes et diadème. Dans une image les jeunes filles qui doivent aller à l'enterrement paraissent maintenues dans un escalier enflammé sous prétexte de leur donner le teint des larmes et l'air de les avoir versées. Il n'y eut pas trois personnes dans l'amphithéâtre du Trocadéro. Ce fut aux organisateurs d'avoir le teint des larmes.
>
> (*20*; p. 83)

If it is accepted that translation and representation are each considered equivalent to something else, namely that the translation is taken to be worth the original and the representation worthy of what it represents, and thus that both are caught up in a system of exchange and value, then the first sentence of this text can be said to present this system of values in such a way as to make it ambiguous. It is as if one were to make an offering and, by that very gesture, cancel the gift. Seats are first offered free of charge (negation of exchange), and then the price of the seats is announced, thereby negating the offer and reinstating exchange. To give seats away free is to remove oneself from the circuit of exchange; to charge for them is precisely to participate in such a circuit.

The style of the text betrays the same ambiguity. The quotation marks surrounding the first sentence imply neither narration nor re-portage: it is more precisely a "gratuitous" utterance addressed directly (by the concerned character) to the world, including the reader. But this "style," no sooner introduced, is replaced by another. "Il s'agit de . . . " implies a narrator who conveys something from another location. From a direct style of address, the text adopts an indirect style and thereby enters a circuit of exchange, of equivalence ("what I relate is equivalent to what I saw"), of representation, and of translation, all of which challenge the direct style. If direct address is the style of the present and of the offering, then indirectness implies the past, re-presentation, and the interest. These two styles and the circuits they imply compose the play (taken again in its systemic sense) of this text: situated at several levels, they vie for primacy; the result is the endless flicker of a kinetic apparatus.

The peculiar atmosphere of this text is announced by its initial element, the title: "Fêtons la mort" (let's celebrate death), which creates an obvious paradox. Then there is the fact that this Russian writer earns glory at his death. This, too, could indicate a paradox, unless it is intended to deride those critics who maintain that a writer achieves glory only after his death. Further, how can a writer earn glory if not through his books? "Entre dans la gloire" could mean to become part of a book. And this is precisely what happens: books are distributed at the feast in which he appears, yet he appears in the book as a dead man, namely, in his present situation. These books, these free prospectuses of the feast, are thus superfluous: they report precisely the events of the "fête" taking place at that moment. They not only focus on the present but on the immediate: they depict the very scene occurring at the Trocadero amphitheater. The narrative in the book converges on the death re-presented in the scene. In fact, the two representations have bookish qualities, that is to say both are stereotypical, neither rings true, both provide local color: Maroussia and Anna, braids and diadems, the *appearance* of having cried. Everything, even the simulation, recapitulates the present—in this case, death—rather than evoke the past life of the writer as is customary in such circumstances. The ending of the poem is thus perfectly coherent. First, because almost no one agrees to take part in this free feast in every sense. Three characters alone (probably Anna, Maroussia, and the Russian) are in the amphitheater; they are the actors *and* the spectators. Nothing more could have been expected from this circuit from which exchange is—or pretends to be—lacking: they *gratuitously* put on a show for *their own* benefit. Yet the poem itself is not gratuitous: following the ambiguity and instability, the conclusion is clearly marked as a "narrative": the use of a literary past tense and the slight distance taken with regard to the rest of the poem permits the resurgence of a narrator, he who proffers the anecdote, the intermediary who reintroduces the exchange.

Although presented more explicitly, a similar type of organization may be found in "Le Soldat de Marathon":

> C'est fête à l'Asile des Aliénistes: les sentiers de ce domaine, la nuit, sont envahis par une foule aimable et un peu craintive. Il y a çà et là de petites tables de bois où une bougie est protégée par un verre et où l'on vend des bonbons: tout s'est passé correctement à ceci près que, pendant la représentation théâtrale donnée par les malades, l'un d'eux qui faisait le rôle d'un sir ou lord quelconque se jetait à terre fréquemment dans une pose célèbre et criait: "C'est moi qui suis le soldat de Marathon!" Il fallait que des gens à coupe-file vinssent le rappeler à la raison, au présent, aux présences, aux préséances, mais il n'osaient se servir du bâton à cause du présent, des présences, des préséances.
>
> *(36; p. 116)*

Facilitated by the proximity of the two expressions: "insane asylum" and "alienists' asylum," the dissonance provoked by the latter is quickly repressed. In fact, we have little choice but to perform this repression if we are to read and understand what follows: the aberrant topic must be transformed in order for us to listen to the commentary. The reader, in other words, must play; he must pretend not to note the anomaly—no doubt a question of "préséances" ("precedences"). The following lines justify this expedient: the poem deals with an insane—and not an insanist—asylum toward which a crowd is moving to attend a celebration. Everything along the way prepares and leads to this conclusion: the concession stands selling candies reinforce the atmosphere of genuine festivity. This movement toward an asylum is confirmed by another detail: on the tables are "candles . . . protected by glasses." This type of glass, according to the Littré dictionary, is also called an "asylum," an asylum from the "invading" wind. A certain schema is established and repeated: just as the candles are protected in an asylum, so too are the madmen in an asylum to be protected from the outside world—and not vice versa. The day of celebration at the asylum is thus a day of interference. The poem itself is, in many respects, a poem about interference: not only of the outside world with the asylum, but also in the midst of the celebration, in the midst of the theatrical "représentation," and, finally, in the midst of the language of the text.

The three words "présent, présences, préséances" echo the word "représentation" used earlier, and, in so doing, qualify and modify it. As a re-presentation it is, first, a present offered and presented by the insane to the audience. But it is also a *re*-presentation, something which was given to the madmen and which they now return, something such as the role of a "sir" or a "lord," which does not come from them or from their domain but from without, and which they now re-present to that same outside world. The incompatibility of the role with the madmen is clearly articulated by the text: "one of them . . . acting *the part of a sir or a lord*," as in the expression to "act crazy" or "to act like an idiot." In this instance, "acting the part of" means to play at playing: another second-degree representation which must be understood as a madman playing the part of an actor playing the part of a sir or lord—a kind of miniature Marat/Sade.

The notion of interference permeates the text: interference of the external with the internal, in the form of outsiders in the asylum and in the form of this re-presentation of a play from without—almost as if it were not an asylum. Further interference occurs within the preceding forms as a madman plays a role inappropriate to this play: he acts as the soldier of Marathon. More precisely, he does not act at all: rather than play a player, he becomes that soldier. And this constitutes an interference with regard to the "préséances" imposed by the "présences" of the outside world. His declaration, "It is I, the soldier of Marathon," is both a negation of the first and second degree representations, and the affirmation of the madman's true identity: "I am the true messenger; the rest is but noise: representations of representations."

His being the soldier of Marathon is justified in another respect: the "normal" representation, by calling upon him to be a sir or a lord, makes a metonymic appeal to his personal fantasies: from lord to soldier. He appears on the scene of his own fantasies and offers, presents (no longer re-presents) them to the disconcerted audience. Stated in the vocabulary of translation, the soldier's "scene" is a vestige of the original version which failed to be translated in accordance with the "présences" and "préséances." He *is* the soldier of Marathon and cannot be dissuaded from this stance. Attempts are made to recall him to "reason," when in fact he is being asked to be twice as mad by playing an actor who plays. They want to recall him to the "present" (in both the sense of temporality and gift), when in fact he is already there: he offers something authentic, something that is not a recycled version of some past; his scene is entirely rooted in the present. They want to recall him to the "présences," without realizing that *he* is the only presence: besides him there are madmen playing the parts of others and spectators pretending to attend the theater.

As for the so-called "préséances," these too are apocryphal: transposed from the outside into a context in which, by definition, they do not apply; in pretending that they apply at the asylum, the audience also plays a role. But, upon closer examination, this audience can be seen to have repressed the aberration of a madman who opts to be himself rather than play a role. "Precedences" are precisely what dictate this repression: in order to perpetuate the illusion of attending a theatrical production, in order to continue playing the role of an audience, they must overlook the interference of a soldier on the scene—much like an actor who must speak his lines *as if* his fellow actor had not missed his cue. And this is precisely why the attendants will not use their clubs: they would rupture the folly of both the madman and the audience. The illusion would break down. Thus the audience, which normally delegates to alienists the function of protecting itself from the insane, is caught up in the soldier's circuit: the alienists are the alienated, the theater is a folly, and asking a madman to play is doubly a folly. And when madness interferes with the game, it is the audience that becomes doubly mad.

One final issue remains unresolved, namely, the fact that the soldier on the scene does not repeat the famous line of the original soldier, "We are the victors," but instead insists upon his identity as a soldier and messenger. In other words, his message is no more than the identification of his function; he presents himself as the channel of communication. This situation recalls that of Mercury, the divine postman, whose scepter, the channel of communication, is his only message. By simply announcing his function without transmitting a message, without conveying something from another place or time, without in fact offering that which is absent, the soldier gives once again only that which is entirely present, namely himself, with absolute conviction, or, in my vocabulary, himself, untranslated. But since the audience and we, the readers, know that he is not truly the soldier of Marathon, his play takes the form of a new mask, a pure mask that can only utter its proper name: "Soldier of Marathon." In this sense, the proper name is mask. What then of the poet's own name, Max, which also says "mask," as is clear in the already mentioned aphorism that is found in "Le coq et la perle"?

> M. de Max offrait tous ses profils à chacun des deux partis
> comme autant de prismes géants.
>
> *(12o;* p. 72)

What exactly is the untranslated? The untranslated is, first of all, that which, in a context of translation, a context of the transfer of meaning between two forms, passes unchanged—for whatever reasons. It is that which, in a context of translation, is not translated: where nothing is conveyed from somewhere else, or, inversely, where everything passes so effectively that any form may be appropriated by any meaning (as in the texts concerning Fantomas). The untranslated may also manifest itself in situations of translation in which the conditions intrinsically posed for this translation inhibit the translation; this was the case with "Fêtons la mort," which strives to abolish the temporal and spatial distances between the source-text and the target-text, as it was with "Soldat de Marathon," in which the present erupts into and interferes with the target-text. In each case, the machinery of translation is exposed, at least implicitly, and in each case a different means is implemented to inhibit the functioning of this machinery. The result is a text that reveals both its own machinery and the disruption of that machinery, yet which never yields a positive result: the translation always fails. The result is also a text built upon a well-known foundation that, bit by bit, severs its roots, and floats, unmoored, as a surface without a body. If, for Max Jacob, the mask conceals nothing, then the untranslated translates nothing either. The mask and the untranslated are texts woven on a loom which, once completed, retain only a memory of what engendered them. And it is precisely this vacillation, this unstable give-and-take between present and past, here and there, foundation and surface that lend Max Jacob's poetry the aspects of play.

9

Conclusion: Interplay, Interference, Poetry

In conclusion, I would like to offer an outline that will permit my generalizing about what has tacitly underpinned this study. Throughout my discussion, an unvarying schema has guided my remarks. Whether I was discussing Max Jacob's life, the place of his poetry in the development of the modern text, or the importance of the obstacle and the mask in that poetry, whether I was examining his poems under the heading of one mask or another (riddles, parodies, diversions), or whether I was analyzing the role of communication (or more specifically, translation) in his poetry, I invariably referred to an "in-between." Everything for Max Jacob took place in that space, and my purpose has been only to establish that fact and elaborate upon its implications and ramifications. This "in-between" was identified by different names, each suited to the discussion at hand: in speaking of his life, I referred to "marginality"; I spoke of "front" when attempting to situate his texts; "obstacles," "windows," and "mirrors" were used in a discussion of the relations between that poetry and the world; "mask," "riddle," "parody," "diversion" were the terms adopted to discuss the poet's relation to his text and to the reader; and, finally, "channel of communication" was used in the context of translation.

Each time this in-between *could have* marked the simple, efficacious, and satisfying passage between two points, could have yielded a simple relation that emphasized these points. But this was never the case. On the contrary, each time something intervened in the passage either from the exterior or the interior (that is, from the very constitution of the relation) to deny it the efficacity and the satisfaction it would have brought. In each case, a line obliquely intersected the first, disrupting the type of relation it sought to establish, and depriving the points of a privileged status. As I noted, there was a message to transmit *and* an interference, translation *and* something untranslated, sleight of hand *and* the risk of a real disappearance, a parody *and* its negation through the obliteration of the source-text, a riddle *and* its built-in solution, a window *and* a mirror, a face *and* a mask. Each of these *ands* both negates the relation and creates a new, two-dimensional space that is neither the point of departure nor the point of arrival, yet is a space defined by these points and by their abolition. Max Jacob's poetry takes place in this complex space between the self and the world, between the exterior and the interior.

This complex space is also the space of play. Neither serious nor nonserious, neither real nor imaginary, yet produced by these pairs, it is that space which D. W. Winnicott described as "the intermediate area of experiencing."[1] It is a precarious, potential space stretched like a tightrope between external reality and internal psychic life, between the reality we all share and pure hallucination. It is a transitional space *between* the inside and the outside that permits their interplay. There, man engages in the "never-ending task" of passing from one point to another: an infinite passage which, according to Winnicott, is the essence of play and of culture in general.[2]

This space is also that of interference, which in information theory certainly has its "negative" aspects when considered from a strictly local point of view (the efficacity of the transmission of a message), but which, from a general point of view, has "positive," even vital, properties. For if information theory teaches us that there can be no message transmitted without some loss, the inverse is also true: dissipation, noise, and interference are necessary for there to be a trans-

1. *Playing and Reality* (London: Tavistock, 1971; rpt. London: Penguin Books, 1974), p. 3.
2. Ibid., pp. 112–22.

mission of messages. For the purposes of this discussion, that statement would imply that a loss of the represented is necessary for any representation, and that translation depends upon a transformation. Interference is precisely what permits speech, discourse, and poetry. Balzac in his efforts to achieve "realism" was aware of this; note his persistent references to the inadequacy of even his most seemingly exhaustive descriptions.

A desire to exploit the properties of interference also lies at the base of much so-called modern literature, in particular the writing of Max Jacob: whereas traditional writing based on representation longs to reduce this noise as much as possible, modern writing, on the contrary, strives to expose its necessary inclusion. Such interference takes the form of ambiguity and equivocation in Max Jacob's writing; it accounts for a confusion of the channel of communication with the message, the momentary subversion of the subject-sender or subject-receiver, or even, as is most often the case, the interference between two systems, two orders that are, a priori, different and isolated. Max Jacob's text is situated in the space of this interaction, in this marginality where references interfere with one another, where interplay occurs in the margins. As Michel Serres has said, interference also means "inter-references,"[3] and the objective of Max Jacob's text—as in all interference—is to permit a new order, a new information, and a new reference to emerge from the noise and disorder. At least, this was his goal. It is perhaps beginning to be realized.

And we may begin to look for this information in the area of play, since his text's most persistent suggestion is that today play can no longer be defined paradigmatically, as Johan Huizinga and his predecessors have done, but that, rather, a theory of play must be syntagmatically constructed in order to take into account inter-play, inter-reference, surface, margins, and the rest. Play is a space between two paradigmatic spaces, syntagmatically related to them. . . .

3. *Hermès II: L'interférence* (Paris: Minuit, 1972), pp. 19–65.

I hope that my study has itself helped destabilize the clownish image that Max Jacob has had from the moment he started writing and publishing until now. Max Jacob is a clown, no one can deny it, but his clownishness has implications far beyond the simple description of his personality or the eccentric aspect of his poetry. It is first of all a sign of rapidly increasing change that was occurring at the time that he wrote *Le Cornet*: the First World War, new positions in philosophy, great new discoveries in the sciences, new literary movements, manifestos in art were questioning the foundations of the past century. Rather than espousing new foundations only to leave them shortly afterward, Max Jacob incorporated the lack of foundation itself into his poetry. In that regard, it can perhaps be said that his poetry is historically determined: it is a poetry of instability and ambiguity which was created during a period when the past was being abolished and the future almost totally unknown.

On the personal level, Max Jacob's clownishness is also part of a complex system. As I have noted in the preceding chapters, his game is fundamentally solitary. Both the instability of his play and his solitude have to be taken into account to give a picture of his state of mind. His questioning is interior; he questions the world within him and there can find nothing to grasp and guide him, no esthetic, no belief, no identity. There he finds nothing but transformations, movements, spurious images of oneself. Max Jacob is fundamentally lost within himself. I believe that this solitary instability is a good starting point to explain his conversion to Catholicism. For Max Jacob, religion possibly played the role of an order coming from without which is easily internalized and which, with a strong longing for order, is suddenly believed to be coming from within. Fortunately, religion did not totally stabilize Max Jacob's thinking. To his death he continued to play, and the instability simply shifted areas: it located itself between stability and instability themselves, between the new-found order and play.

Selected Prose and Poetry
from *The Dice Cup*
translated by
Judith Morganroth Schneider

1   1916 Preface

Everything that exists is situated. Everything that is above matter is situated; matter itself is situated. Two works of art are unequally situated either with respect to the minds of their authors or with respect to their devices. Raphael is above Ingres, Vigny above Musset. Madame X— is above her cousin; the diamond is above quartz. Maybe it has something to do with the relation between the morale and morals? In the past people believed that artists were inspired by angels and that there were different categories of angels.

Buffon said: "Style is the man himself." Which means a writer must write with his blood. The definition is salutary; it does not seem accurate to me. What constitutes the man himself is his language, his sensibility; we are right in saying: express yourself in your own words. We are wrong in believing that is style. Why give style in literature a definition other than the one it has in the various arts? Style is the will to exteriorize oneself by chosen means. Like Buffon we generally confuse language and style, because few men need an art of the will, that is, art itself, and because everybody needs humanity in expression. In great artistic epochs, the rules of art taught from childhood constitute canons that provide a style: the artists then are those who, in spite of rules followed since childhood, find a vivid form of expression. This vivid form of expression is the charm of aristocracies, the charm of the seventeenth century. The nineteenth century is full of writers who understood the need for style, but who did not dare descend from the throne built by their desire for purity. They created obstacles for themselves at the expense of life.[1] Once he has situated his work, the author may use every charm: language, rhythm, musicality, and wit. *When a singer has placed his voice in a register, he may amuse himself with vocal flourishes.* To understand me well, compare the familiarities of Montaigne with those of Aristide Bruant or the elbowings of a sensationalist newspaper with the brutalities of Bossuet jostling the Protestants.

This theory is not ambitious, nor is it new: it is the classical theory

---

1. The prose poem must remain, in spite of the rules that refine it, a free and vivid form of expression.

that I humbly recall. The names I cite are not here to pound the "moderns" with the club of the "ancients", they are indisputable names; if I had cited others that I know, you would perhaps have thrown away the book, something I do not desire; I want you to read it not for a long while, but often: to make oneself understood is to make oneself loved. Only long works are esteemed; well now, it is difficult to sustain beauty for long. Someone may even prefer a Japanese poem of three lines to Péguy's *Eve*, which has three hundred pages, and one of Madame de Sévigné's letters full of happiness, audacity, and ease, to one of those novels of former times made of pieces stitched together, which claimed to have done enough for cohesion, if they had satisfied the requirements of their thesis.

Many prose poems have been written in the past thirty or forty years; I know of hardly a poet who understood what it was all about and who managed to sacrifice authorial ambitions to the formal constitution of the prose poem. Dimension is nothing to the beauty of the work, its situation and style are everything. Now, I claim that *The Dice Cup* satisfies the reader from this double point of view.

Artistic emotion is neither a sensorial act, nor a sentimental act; otherwise nature would suffice to provide us with it. Art exists, therefore it corresponds to a need: art is strictly speaking a *distraction*. I am not mistaken: this is the theory that has provided us with a marvelous race of heroes, with powerful evocations of milieus in which the legitimate curiosities and aspirations of the bourgeois, prisoners of themselves, are satisfied. But we must give the word "distraction" a still broader significance. A work of art is a force that attracts, that absorbs the available strength of whoever approaches it. Something like a marriage occurs here and the art-lover plays the part of the woman. He needs to be taken by a will and held. The will thus plays the principal role in creation; the rest is only the bait before the trap. The will can only exercise itself on the choice of means, because the work of art is simply an ensemble of means and, for art, we arrive at the definition that I gave of style: art is the will to exteriorize oneself by chosen means: the two definitions coincide and art is simply style. Style is here considered the setting of materials into a work and the composition of the ensemble, not the language of the writer. And I conclude that artistic emotion is the effect of a thinking action directed toward a thought action. I use the word "thinking" regretfully, for I am convinced that artistic emotion ceases where analysis and thought intervene: it is one thing to provoke reflection and another to provide the emotion of beauty. I put thought with the bait before the trap.

The greater the activity of the subject, the more emotion provided by the object increases; thus the work of art must be distanced from the subject. That is why it has to be *situated*. We might here refute Baudelaire's theory of surprise: that theory is rather obvious. Baudelaire understood the word "distraction" in its most ordinary sense. To surprise is not much, one must *transplant*. Surprise charms and prevents true creation: it is harmful like all charms. A creator has the right to be charming only after the event, when the work is situated and styled.

Let us distinguish the style of a work from its situation. Style or will creates, that is, it separates. Situation distances, that is, it stimulates artistic emotion; we recognize that a work has style by the fact that it gives the impression of being closed; we recognize that it is situated by the little shock we receive or else by the margin surrounding it, by the special atmosphere in which it moves. Certain of Flaubert's works have style, not one is situated. Musset's theater is situated and does not have much style. Mallarmé's work is the model of the situated work: if Mallarmé were not so affected and obscure, he would be a great classic. Rimbaud has neither style, nor situation: he has Baudelairean surprise; he is the triumph of Romantic disorder.

Rimbaud extended the scope of our sensibility and every literary man must be grateful to him for that, but authors of prose poems cannot take him as their model, for the prose poem in order to exist must submit to the laws of all art, which are style or will and situation or emotion, and Rimbaud leads only to disorder and exasperation. The prose poem must also avoid Baudelairean and Mallarméean parables, if it would distinguish itself from the fable. It is probably clear that I do not regard as prose poems those notebooks containing more or less quaint impressions published from time to time by my colleagues who have a surplus of material. A page of prose is not a prose poem, even if it encloses two or three lucky finds. I would consider as such those so-called finds presented with the necessary spiritual margin. In connection with this point, I warn authors of prose poems to avoid excessively brilliant gems that attract the eye at the expense of the ensemble. The poem is a constructed object and not a jeweler's window. Rimbaud is the jeweler's window, not the jewel: the prose poem is a jewel.

A work of art receives validity from itself and not from any possible comparison with reality. We say at the movies: "That's it exactly!" We say before an object of art: "What harmony! What solidity! What cohesion! What purity!" The cute definitions of Jules Renard fall flat in front of this truth. They are realistic works, without real existence; they have style, but are not situated; the same charm that gives them life, kills them. I believe Jules Renard has written prose poems other than his definitions: I am sorry I do not know them: he may be the inventor of the genre as I conceive it. For the moment, I consider as such Aloysius Bertrand and the author of the *Book of Monelle*, Marcel Schwob. Both have style and margin: that is, they compose and they situate. I reproach one of them for his Romanticism "after Callot," as he says, which, by drawing attention to colors that are too violent, veils the work itself. It must be added, as he declared, that in his judgment, his pieces were materials for a work and not in themselves clearly defined works. I reproach the other author for his having written tales and not poems, and what tales! precious, puerile, artistic! Yet it could be that these two writers created the genre of the "prose poem" without even knowing it.

September 1916   Max Jacob

2   A Brief Historical Account of *The Dice Cup*

To my friend Paul Bonet.

"Oh what a title!" Miss Hastings (an English lady writer and Modigliani's woman) would say, "in England, you know, they'd steal it from you before the book appeared!" Something else indeed was stolen! The poems were well known! They'd all come over in the morning, to number 7, rue Ravignan, to read the poem of the night before . . . the neighbors, Picasso, Salmon, MacOrlan, etc. "There'll be some poaching in there!" MacOrlan would say; and, as a matter of fact, when the question of publishing came up, someone whom I won't name hurriedly got out a collection, under another title (for all that we're not in London) which pretended to be a pastiche and didn't succeed. Loud ovation from the gang! "Down Max!" and I myself asking Picasso: "Is it true that X— is better than I?" "You know very well that the imitator is always better than the inventor!" That was a way of sitting on the fence and the truth. Nonetheless X—'s book has fallen into oblivion while the little "Cup" is alive and well. There were two editions published by Stock (little yellow books) and after the one that was put out on subscription, by the author, at 17, rue Gabriel, Paris 18, I remember a letter from Albert Thibaudet, then a soldier in the War Ministry: "It's as if all the files had fallen pell-mell on my desk." Laurent Tailhade, informed by a sidekick, deigned to comment: "Dahlia! dahlia! that Delila tied." All the same I had a good deal of success.

I've always invented prose or half-prose poems. When my five brothers and sisters and I, as young children, would come home from the traveling circus, in the night, escorted by the maid, we'd be very frightened in the stairway without automatic lighting, and I'd improvised this: "Mr. Cat and Mr. Robber, if there are cats and if there are robbers, Mr. Cat, don't scratch! Mr. Robber, don't make me shudder!"

Surely, there's the *Cup* already; was I twelve or fifteen years old?

Later, as a student in Paris, I used to visit some prominent rich cousins and I'd made this up: "My overcoat is my shield, my umbrella is my defender, I've won 50 cents from my enemies, by chance, and you, Miss, you know how to dance!" I was completely unaware of Jarry and Père Ubu at the time; besides, there was no question of literature yet in my life.

Later, after some previous affairs, there I was a clerk at 137 Boulevard Voltaire, and in possession of a young woman; we were living at 33 Boulevard Barbès; I said to her one day: "She's so weary that the eyelids of the buttercups on her hat are closing." But it wasn't until still later, after it had been established that I was one of the poets (and quoted in the famous "afternoon of the poets," a lecture given by Apollinaire at the Independents' Show in 1907, I'm exaggerating, I'd been collecting prose poems for a long while) that I made a serious effort to seize from within myself, and by every means possible, the data of the unconscious: liberated words, chance associations of ideas, day and night dreams, hallucinations, etc.

"Why don't you do a sequel to *The Dice Cup*?" Count François de Gouy d'Arcy asked me. (He's the only man who knows what painting is, Picasso used to say of him,) "Do one for me!" So I set about it; one day, into the telephone, I announced that I had sixty pages. "Come to dinner! and bring the sixty pages"; they were read with enthusiasm, friends were called on the telephone, and at each new arrival, they had to be read once again. After midnight, my arms full of flowers, I was driven by the chauffeur to 17, rue Gabriel, my domicile. The smallest farthing would have suited me better.

Some time afterwards, François telephoned me to say that he and his friend Greeley had discovered a little spot near Versailles from which you could see all of Paris "and that atmosphere touched with gold." "Right," I said, "and it's not only the atmosphere that has the golden touch." This allusion was understood, and François began to complain about his poverty and his snatched inheritance, etc. Evening came, then night. This happened in a hotel near the Place de l'Etoile. "What time is it?" said François. "Two o'clock by that lovely antique watch." "You like this watch? take it!" For over ten years I've worn that watch on holidays and at ceremonies: I even attached it to a long gold chain. — Today I'm thinking about selling it; what's the point, when you live like a hermit, of owning jewelry? (the same goes for my emerald) it's a matter of fifteen thousand francs, an amount that will last at least as long as my waning life and alleviate certain little cares. Never will *The Dice Cup* itself earn me as much as its supplement. Filibuth is part of the business, too, for my prospective buyer wants to have the watch as a souvenir of that novel whose subtitle is "Filibuth; or, The Gold Watch."

1943

3 1914   His bulging stomach is stand-offishly corseted. His plumed hat is flat; his face is a gruesome skull, only brown and so ferocious that you'd expect to see some sort of rhinoceros horn or superfluous tooth protruding from his terrifying maxillary. O sinister vision of German death.

4 War   The boulevards on the edge of the city, at night, are covered with snow; the bandits are soldiers; they attack me with laughs and sabers, they strip me: I escape only to fall into another square. Is it the courtyard of a barracks, or of an inn? how many sabres! how many lancers! it's snowing! someone gives me an injection with a syringe: it's a poison to kill me; a death's head veiled in crepe bites my finger. Looming streetlamps are projecting the light of my death on the snow.

5 False News! Funeral News!   At the opera, at a performance of *For the Crown*, as Desdemona sang "My father is in Goritz and my heart in Paris," a shot was heard from a box in the fifth balcony, then a second from the orchestra, and instantly rope ladders were unwound; a man tried to climb down from the top of the house: a bullet stopped him at the level of the balcony. All the spectators were armed and it turned out that the house was packed with nothing but . . . and . . . Then, there were assassinations of neighbors, volleys of liquid fire. There were sieges of boxes, the siege of the stage, the siege of a folding seat and the battle raged for eighteen days. Perhaps the two sides were replenished, I can't say, but what I do know for sure is that the newsmen came for such a gory sight, and that one of them, being ill, sent his respected mother, who took quite an interest in the coolness of a young French gentleman who held out for eighteen days in a stage-box without consuming anything but a little broth. This episode of the Balcony Wars did a good deal for voluntary enlistments in the provinces. And, on the banks of my river, under my trees, I know of three brothers in brand-new uniforms who embraced each other with dry eyes, while their families looked for sweaters in the attic closets.

6 In Search of the Traitor   Another hotel! my friend Paul is a prisoner of the Germans. My God, where is he? Lautenbourg, that's a furnished hotel, rue Saint-Sulpice, but I don't know the room number! the hotel desk is a pulpit too lofty for my eyes. I'd like to, would you have a Miss Cypriani . . . it must be room 21 or 26 or 28 and there I go dreaming of the cabalistic significance of those ciphers. Meanwhile Paul is a prisoner of the Germans for having betrayed his colonel: in what epoch are we living? 21, 26, 28 are ciphers painted in white along with three keys on a black background. Who is Miss Cypriani? another spy.

7 Poem in a Manner That Is Not Mine
To you, Baudelaire

Through the leaves of a holly bush appeared a city, and nearby, Don Juan, Rothschild, Faust, and a painter were chatting.

"I've amassed a great fortune," said Rothschild, "and, since it has given me no pleasure, kept on acquiring wealth, hoping to recapture the joy I felt at my first million."

"And I've kept on looking for love amidst misfortunes," said Don Juan. "To be loved and not to love is pure torture; but I keep on looking for love, hoping to recapture the emotion of my first love."

"When I found the secret of success," said the painter, "I sought other secrets in order to occupy my mind; but those secrets did not bring me the same success as the first one and so I've come back to my original formula even though I'm sick of it."

"And I gave up seeking knowledge in exchange for happiness," said Faust, "but I've come back to seeking knowledge, even though my methods are outdated, because there is no other happiness than seeking."

Beside them was a young woman wearing a crown of artificial ivy, who said:

"I'm bored, I'm too beautiful!"

And from behind the holly bush God said: "I know the universe, I'm bored."

8 Poem   "What wilt thou of me," said Mercury.

"Your smile and your teeth," said Venus.

"They are false. What wilt thou of me?"

"Your caduceus."

"I never part with it."

"Come, bring it here, divine postman."

That must be read in the original Greek: it is called an *Idyll*. In preparatory school, a friend, often failed in his exams, said to me: "If someone translated a novel of Daudet into Greek, he'd be well prepared for the exam! but I can't work at night. It makes my mother cry!" That, too, must be read in the original Greek, gentlemen: it is an idyll, εἰδυλλος, a picturesque description.

9 Poem   Scratch out the heads of the imperial generals! But they're alive! all I can do is change their hats: the hats are full of gun cotton and these gentlemen of the Empire don't fool around: gun cotton catches fire. I didn't know gun cotton was such a snow-white pigeon. Enter this biblical landscape! but it's a woodcut: an uneven row of houses, a strand behind a thin jet of water, a thin jet of water behind a palm tree. An illustration for *Saint Matorel*, a novel by Max Jacob. Miss Leona and I: we're taking a stroll there, I didn't know we carried suitcases in this book! The generals seated at that banquet were alive under their hats, but then, Miss Leona and I, aren't we? I can't enter this biblical landscape, it's a woodcut: I even know the engraver. When the hats of the imperial generals had been put back on, everything was in order; I reentered the woodcut and calm reigned in the desert of art.

10 Poem   When the boat had reached the islands of the Indian Ocean, someone noticed they had no maps. They would have to go ashore! It was then that they recognized who was on board: that sanguinary man who gives his wife tobacco and takes it back. The islands were sown in every direction. At the top of the cliff, they saw small Negroes wearing derby hats: "Maybe they'll have maps!" We took the cliff path: it was a rope ladder: along the ladder maybe there were maps! even Japanese maps! we kept climbing. Finally, when there were no more rungs (ivory crabs, somewhere) we had to climb by our wrists. My brother, the African, gave a good account of himself; as for me, I discovered rungs where there weren't any. Once at the top, we're on a wall; my brother jumps. I myself am at the window! I'll never be able to make up my mind to jump: it's a wall of red planks: "Go round," shouts my brother, the African. There are no more floors, nor passengers, nor boat, nor small Negro; there's the round to make. What round? how discouraging.

11 The Tree Gnawers   Alone, or imprisoned, or working, Alexander Dumas *père* would console himself with the odor of an article of clothing belonging to a woman. Three identical men, same round hat, same short build, finding themselves equally amazed at their identity, suddenly read in each other's thoughts an identical idea: to steal the lonely man's consolation.

12 The Rooster and the Pearl

12a   I declare myself universal, oviparous, a giraffe, parched, sinophobic, and hemispheric. I quench my thirst at the springs of the atmosphere which laughs concentrically and farts at my uncertainty.

12b   Those white arms became my entire horizon.

12c   When you paint a picture, at each stroke, it changes entirely, turning like a cylinder and appearing almost interminable. When it stops turning, it's finished. My latest represented a tower of Babel made out of lighted candles.

12d   Augustine was a farm girl when the President noticed her. To avoid a scandal, he bestowed upon her titles and teaching certificates, then a "Lady" before her name, some money, and the more he provided for her, the more worthy of him she became. Poor Breton peasant, I've given myself everything, the title of duke, the right to wear a monocle, I've managed to aggrandize my height, my thought, and still I can't become worthy of myself.

12e   There's no longer anything but the tops of the trees, there's no longer anything but the edge of a roof of a house, there's no longer anything but a sick buttock, that makes a false allegation in order to get at the truth and is right.

12f   The infant, the efant, the elephant, the frog, and the sautéed potato.

12g   Fog, spider's orb.

12h   It was a percale Pierrot costume, with trousers too short even to cover the knee, that I rented, arguing over it with a certain sergeant. In the costume I found some letters! yes! letters that I'll publish when the shop is destroyed or the sergeant dead.

12i   Wall of bricks, abode of books!

12j   Between the curtains, the lintel is a slide for the smoke! no! for the dancing blue angels.

12k   The sun is made of gilt-edged lace.

12l   You are like an irascible bread and milk soup foaming under the airship, mountains, and, from there, soon emerges, as if from a gigantic dice cup, the good old globe, the forehead of Father Double Sphere.

12m   On occasion, a fish while it's swimming
Shows the waves its white underpinning
While the airship, a fish that goes flying,
Presents a white view to the clouds,
The dancer, as she goes spinning,
On stage will display to the seated crowds
A spine slimy with diamonds all glittering.

12n   A diadem is changed into a thousand Deputies' heads.

12o   Monsieur de Max showed each of the two sides all of his profiles in turn, like so many giant prisms.

13 Frontispiece   Yes, it fell from the button of my breast and I didn't even notice. Like a boat and its sailors leaving the anchorage of the rock without multiplying the ripples of the sea, without the earth sensing this new adventure, there fell from my Cybelline breast a new poem and I didn't even notice.

14 Moon Poem   Against the night are three mushrooms that are the moon. As abruptly as the cuckoo clock strikes, they re-arrange themselves each month at midnight. In the garden are rare flowers that are little prone men, a hundred of them, reflections in a mirror. In my dark room is a luminous incense holder, that prowls about, then two . . . phosphorescent airships, reflections in a mirror. In my head is a bee that is speaking.

15 Poem from the Java of Mr. René Ghil and
     Called the Ksours   With a scratch of the fingernail, the women push in the folds of their lids to give their eyes the look of statues. No one has the right to sleep here any more. Those who have café au lait eyes like their stags serve . . . Oh! thy diadem coral phallus, Tao-Phen-Tsu! . . . They will not be forgotten. Three dwarfs, navy officers, descended the champagne-colored precipice to make boulalaika, with some hetaerae from the Champagne re-gion, and, that night, two schoolboys left their . . . (here a brief dis-order which is not unbecoming) to play a duet on painted noisemak-ers under the covered playground of those . . . electric. With a scratch of the fingernail, they push in the folds of their lids to give their eyes the look of statues, but those who have eyes like sugar virgins never want to be touched. Someone is singing in that cicada tongue and the prince-gods are eating bread and jam from the tips of their fingernails.

16 Infernal Night   Something dreadfully cold falls on my shoulders. Something gluey sticks to my neck. From out of the heavens comes a voice crying: "Monster!" and I don't know whether it means me or my vices or, for that matter, if it's referring to the viscous creature sticking to my neck.

17 Rue Ravignan   "You never bathe twice in the same stream," the philosopher Heraclitus used to say. And yet, it's always the same ones who come back up! At the same time of day, they pass by, gay or sad. To all of you, passersby of the rue Ravignan, I have given the names of History's defunct! Now here comes Agamemnon! and here's Madame Hanska! Ulysses is the milkman! Patroclus is down at the bottom of the street while Pharaoh is up here near me. Castor and Pollux are the fifth-floor ladies. But you, old ragpicker, you, who, in the fairy-like morn, come to collect the still living scraps as I put out my good stout lamp, you whom I do not know, mysterious and poor ragpicker, you, ragpicker, I have named you with a noble and celebrated name, I have named you Dostoyevsky.

18 Christmas Story   To Madame Sylvette Olin

Once upon a time there was an architect or else a horse: it was a horse rather than an architect, in Philadelphia, who had been told: "Do you know the cathedral of Cologne? build a cathedral just like the cathedral of Cologne!" And since he did not know the cathedral of Cologne, he was then put in prison. But, in prison, an angel appeared to him, saying: "Wolfrang! Wolfrang! why so sad?" "I must remain in prison, because I don't know the cathedral of Cologne!" "You need Rhine wine to build the cathedral of Cologne, but show them the plan, then you'll be able to get out of prison." And the angel gave him the plan, and he showed them the plan, and then he was able to get out of prison, but he was never able to build the cathedral, because he did not find the Rhine wine. He got the idea of having Rhine wine sent to Philadelphia, but they sent him an atrocious French Moselle instead, so that he could not build the cathedral of Cologne in Philadelphia; he only built an atrocious Protestant church.

19 Translated from the German or the Bosnian   To Madame Edouard Fillacier

My horse is halting! Halt your mount as well, companion, I'm afraid! between the slopes of the hill and ourselves, the turfed slopes of the hill, there's a woman, if it isn't a great cloud. Halt! she's calling me! she's calling me and I see her breast heaving! her arm is beckoning me to follow, her arm . . . if her arm isn't a cloud.

"Halt, companion, I'm afraid, halt! between the trees on the hill, the bowed trees on the hill, I saw an eye, if that eye isn't a cloud. It's staring at me, it unnerves me; halt! It's following our steps on the road, if that eye isn't a cloud."

"Listen, my companion! phantoms, lives of this earth or another, let's not speak of these creatures in the city so that we won't be treated as importunates."

20 Let's Celebrate Death   "I'm going to give you seats free of charge! that'll be two francs fifty!" They're for a celebration at the Trocadero to rejoice in the death of a famous Russian writer who's gone to glory. Someone is distributing guidebooks, one is made of wood carved in a childlike style and the other is illustrated in color. The death of the Russian is represented by a mauve blouse struck by lightning, while Maroussia and Anna bend over him in full national dress: braids and diadems. In one image the young girls who are supposed to go to the funeral appear suspended in a flaming stairwell under the pretext of giving them tear-stained complexions and the look of having shed some. There were not even three people in the amphitheater of the Trocadero. Now it was the organizers' turn to have tear-stained complexions.

21 Double Life   The château has two pointed towers and we stretch out on the hillock across the way. The old spinster looks like a high altar; the steps of the château look like a high altar and here they come flying toward us supported by doves. Now, this high altar was dropping handbills: *Charity Sale*. And the old spinster offered me one without noticing that I had more right to be sold than seller, bought than buyer, and beneficiary than benefactor.

22 A Bit of Art Criticism   Jacques Claes is truly a name for a Dutch painter. Let us, if you will, look briefly into his origins. Young Jacques' mother, as she herself admitted, used to bleach her face with vinegar, which explains why the master's paintings have a varnished air. In Jacques' village, on the day of the Feast

of the Holy Roofer, it was the custom of the roofers to drop down from the rooftops without crushing the passersby, they were also expected to throw ropes from the sidewalks to the chimneys. A very picturesque ensemble which, surely, must have given our painter his taste for the picturesque.

23 Cubism and Sun Drowning

L'eglisiglia del Amore, l'odore del Tarquino, in short, all the monuments of Rome on a *bouteglia* of wine and the corresponding record show that we have drunk copiously, but that we shall abstain: the beaker of the beak and the spout with the watery savor. If we have to repent, we might as well abstain. The volatile rainbow is nothing other than a volcanic decoration in the corner of the label. Mum's the word! and to compare one litre with another: *el spatio del Baccio* and the *Bacco nel cor.*

24 The Success of Confession

On the road leading to the racetrack, there was a beggar who looked like a servant: "Take pity," he said, "I'm corrupt, I'll go gambling with the money you give me." And so forth with his confession. He had great success and he deserved it.

25 Serial Novel

Just then, a car stopped in front of the hotel in Chartres. Now who was in that car, in front of that hotel, was it Toto, was it Totel, that's what you'd like to know, but you'll never know . . . never. . . . The hotelkeepers of Chartres have derived considerable benefit from the frequent visits of Parisians, but these frequent visits to the hotelkeepers of Chartres have done considerable harm to the Parisians for certain reasons. A bellboy took the boots belonging to the owner of the car and polished them: these boots were badly polished, for the abundance of cars at the hotels kept the help from making the arrangements necessary for good boot polishing; quite happily, the same abundance kept our hero from noticing that his boots were badly polished. What was our hero doing in that old citadel of Chartres, which is so renowned? he came looking for a doctor, because there are not enough of them in Paris for the number of ailments he had.

26 The Cygnet (In the Genre of the Witty Essay)

The cygnet is hunted in Germany, the homeland of Lohengrin. It signals a detachable collar in urinals. On lakes, it is confused with flowers and people go into ecstasies, then, over its boatlike shape; furthermore, they mercilessly kill it to hear its song. The art of painting would willingly utilize the cygnet, but we have no more art of painting. When it has had time to change into a woman before dying, its flesh is less tough than in the contrary case: hunters then prize it more highly. Under the name of eider, cygnets aided eiderdown. And that suits it rather well. Men who have long necks like Fénelon, the cygnet of Cambrai, are called cygnet-men or insignia men. Etc.

27 Nocturne of Family Hesitations

There are nights that end in a train station! There are train stations that end in nights. And how many tracks have we crossed in the night! I myself have been knocked about at night by the outer corners of railroad cars: my deltoid still aches at the thought. Waiting for your older sister, or father, in the end the unmentionable always happens: the pair of shoes sprinkled with bread flour. But I have a brother who's really disagreeable in a train station: he arrives at the last minute (he has his principles), then we have to reopen a suitcase that a servant had not brought until now; even at the ticket window, he still doesn't know to which station he ought to direct the cars: he's hesitating between Nogent-sur-Marne and the Ponts-de-Cé or others. There's the suitcase, open! He hasn't obtained his ticket and the gas lamps try in vain to transform the night into day or the day into night. There are nights that end in a train station, train stations that end in the night. Ah! cursed hesitation, it's you isn't it, who's ruined me, and somewhere else indeed than in your waiting rooms, O train stations!

28 Fantomas

On the burnished silver door knocker, sullied by time, sullied by the dust of time, a kind of engraved Buddha with a forehead that is too high, with hanging ears, with the looks of a sailor or a gorilla: it was Fantomas. He was pulling on two cords in order to hoist up I don't know what. His foot slips; his life is at stake;

he must reach the knob of the bell, the rubber knob before the rat who'll riddle it with holes. Now, all that is only silver engraved for a door knocker.

29 Fantomas Again

They were as condescending as they were connoisseurs, the lady and the gentleman. The first time the chef came out from the kitchen, cap in hand, to ask them: "Excuse me, but are the lady and gentleman satisfied?" they answered: "You'll find out from the head waiter!" The second time, they didn't answer. The third time, they considered firing him, but they couldn't make up their minds to it, for he was a unique chef. The fourth time (my God, they lived on the outskirts of Paris, they were always alone, they were so bored!) the fourth time, they began: "The caper sauce is splendid, but the fried bread under the partridge was a bit hard." They began to talk sports, politics, religion. That's exactly what the chef wanted, for he was none other than Fantomas.

30 Untitled

The rose-colored glass case was painted so that it might have been taken for mahogany. The jewels it contained had been stolen, then returned, but by whom? "What do you think?" my mother asked. I looked at the jewels: several clasps, some ornamented with stones, others with miniature water-colors: "I think the thief's insulting us! he gives us back our jewels because they're worthless. I would have done as much." "That thief is an honest man," said my mother, "while you . . . "

31 Paws or Paste

Beside the fireplace, against the wall, that fellow who has a red velvet top hat and a trace of white on his cheek lets me know that he saw Sarah Bernhardt shave her face. It's unbelievable! some sailor from Belle-Îsle apparently surprised her while, imagining herself somewhere in the wilderness, she smoothed out her wrinkles with a paw or paste.

32 Popular Novel

I haven't much longer to go. I've got to answer the examining magistrate on behalf of my friend. Where are the keys? they're not in the chest. Excuse me, your Honor, I've got to look for the keys. Here they are! and what a situation for the judge! Madly in love with the sister-in-law, he was about to give up handling the affair, when she appeared begging him to declare a nonsuit and she'd be all his. The judge, at heart, is bored with the whole affair. He gets bogged down in details: why all these drawings? I plunge headlong into a regular lecture on esthetics. An artist always searches for forms in the many works around him. Night is falling; the judge doesn't understand! he's talking about fraudulent imitations. Some friends arrive. The wife of the accused suggests we all go for a ride, in an automobile, and the judge accepts, hoping that the accused will manage to escape.

33 A Valiant Soldier on Foreign Soil

Olga de Berchold has gone off to Army camp to join the one she loves: Private Verchoud. The soldier goes off to war. Olga follows him enduring hardships along the way. Verchoud is taken prisoner. Olga leaves to sell her assets and returns to pay his ransom: she doesn't hand it over all at once for fear of a trick. The ransom paid, Verchoud falls ill. Olga cares for him and, for the very first time, declares her love. The soldier tells her that she's not the one he loves, that it's a certain peasant girl he's only caught a glimpse of and to whom he's never even spoken. He dies. Olga is ruined, desperate: what will become of her? she sets out to find the peasant girl.

34 At the Chauffeurs' Meeting Place

Our women were sitting on the other bench against the wall. I recognized my place by the books and the papers. I recognized the dawn by the house across the way, but I couldn't understand how it could be so early or so late. We'd talked of a book named *The Little Geese*, by Herrmayer, and of its author named Cabalis or Andral. His pseudonym is Herrmayer: it's a brilliant book. We stole some canned desserts from the restaurant owner. There were dried figs left on the plates of those who don't like grapes, but, as we were stealing some canned desserts, a voice said: "Oh no! not that! hey! That's my chef's apron and my bedsheets."

35 The Key   When the lord of Framboisy came home from the wars, his wife reproached him roundly in church, so he said: "Madame, here is the key to all my worldly possessions, I am leaving forever." The lady tactfully let the key fall to the stone floor of the temple. A nun, in a corner, was praying, because she had lost hers, the key to the convent and no one could get in. "Well, go and see if your lock works with this one." But the key was gone. It was already in the Cluny Museum: it was an enormous key in the shape of a tree trunk.

36 The Soldier of Marathon   It's a holiday at the Alienists' Asylum: the paths of the grounds, at night, are overrun by a friendly and slightly fearful crowd. Here and there are little wooden tables with candles protected by glasses where candy is being sold: everything has gone smoothly except for this, that during the dramatic performance given by the patients, one of them who was acting the part of some Sir or Lord repeatedly threw himself to the ground in a celebrated pose shouting: "It is I, the soldier of Marathon!" Certain persons with passes had to come up and bring him back to his senses, to the present, to the presences, to the precedences, but they didn't dare use a stick because of the present, the presences, and the precedences.

37 Ariste Art   The newspaper *Fémina* describes the mansion of the duchess of H— as a sad barracks of a place and gives a drawn-out description of the greyish red pavingstones of the court-yard. He says that the central room is inhabited by an old servant who watches over the mansion, in summer. What astonishes him is that the curtains always trail along the floor like a dress with a train and he confesses that, being a novelist himself, he looked carefully at everything and even at the other mansions in the neighborhood in which the curtains also trail along the floor. He was witness to a scene or half-scene between the mother and daughter over a matter of physics or fireworks, the maid having asked if there was much physics or fireworks in the boarding school where her own son was sent. There was a slap applied like a certain round leaf, resembling watercress, and growing on walls. I spoke of the servant who guards the mansion, in summer. It is this servant who is in charge of draining. The duchess has an aristocratic profile and the plant on the high wall is called aristolochia, the author of the news report is named Aristides.

38 The Soul of *La Gioconda*

Il Giocondo! That's the baroness's alarm clock. It has the soul of *La Gioconda*, it stops or goes according to the adventures of that unfortunate painting. The police might have consulted it, in the past, it would have answered in the way that certain tables answer their faithful. This piece of clockwork comes from Florence or the Black Forest: it is housed in a mahogany and copper colonnade and never leaves the traveling baroness. It rings, the beautiful lady awakens and thinks. They say that the soul of *La Gioconda* inspires the baronness's lovely poems and paintings and that its mainspring will break forever when she decides to take a new lover. *Il Giocondo* does not have to be wound to continue its clock-like round; however, the chambermaid secretly assists with the magic. Nobody assists with the baronness's magic, except for *La Gioconda* herself, whose mysterious smile keeps watch through the night at her bedside.

39 The Beggar Woman of Naples

When I lived in Naples, at the gate of my palace there was a beggar woman to whom I would toss a few coins before getting into my carriage. One day, surprised at never having received any thanks whatsoever, I looked at the beggar woman. Now, as I looked, I saw that what I had taken for a beggar woman was in fact a wooden box painted green that contained some red earth and a few half-rotten bananas . . .

40 Capital. Table Cover

The little girl's breasts are too far apart, that really ought to be treated in Paris: later on, it would be vulgar. But in Paris all the shops are alike: gold and crystal: specialists for hats! Specialists for watches! Where is the specialist for breasts?

41 Little Poem

I remember my childhood room. The muslin of the curtains covering the windowpane was crisscrossed with white trim, in which I would try to find the alphabet and when I had the letters, I would transform them into imaginary drawings. H, a man seated; B, the arch of a bridge over a river. In the room were several chests with blossomy flowers delicately carved on their wood. But what I preferred were the round tops of two pilasters that were available behind the curtains and that I considered jumping-jack heads with which it was forbidden to play.

42 Metempsychosis

Here darkness and silence! the pools of blood are shaped like clouds. Bluebeard's seven wives are no longer in the cupboard. Nothing remains of them but this organdy coif. But there! there! on the Ocean, there come seven galleys, seven galleys whose ropes hang down from the topsail to the sea like braids on the shoulders of women. They're getting closer! they're getting closer! they're here!

43 The Real Downfall

When I was young, I believed that genii and fairies took the trouble to guide me, and no matter what insult I was paid, I kept on believing that someone prompted others with words whose only intent was my well-being and mine alone. The realities and the disaster that have made me a singer in this square are teaching me that I've always been abandoned by the gods. O genii, o fairies! give me back my illusion, today.

44 The Bibliophile

The binding of the book is a gilt lattice holding captive cockatoos of a thousand colors, boats with postage-stamp sails, sultanas wearing paradises on their heads to show how rich they are. The book holds captive heroines who are poor, steamboats that are soot black, and poor grey sparrows. The author is a head held captive by a tall white wall (I'm referring to the front of his shirt).

45 Heavenly Mystery

Upon returning from the ball, I sat down at the window and contemplated the heavens: it seemed to me that the clouds were enormous heads of old men seated at a table and that someone was bringing them a white bird with its feathers trimmed. A great river cut across the sky. One of the old men lowered his eyes toward me, he was about to speak, when the enchantment dissipated, leaving the pure twinkling stars.

46 Latude — Attitude   A great deal has been written about the case of Latude, the truth has not been written. It was in order to protect herself from her own heart that Madame de Pompadour, that gracious Napoleon of love, ordered the small blue and white officer locked up in the Bastille. Latude escapes! Where does he go? to the land of Spinoza. But there he realized that the taste for meditation is satisfied only in towers and so he returned to his casket of love.

47 Ruses of the Demon to Recover His Prey
The somber wharf, triangular like a turret mast, staked with plane trees in winter, skeletons that are far too pretty on the indented sky. At the inn where we stayed, there was a beautiful, though flat, woman, who hid her hair under a wig or black satin. One day on top of the granite, she appeared to me in the broad daylight of the sea: too tall—like the rocks of the region—she was putting on her shirt, I saw that she was a man and I said so. That night on a sort of London wharf I was punished: watch out for the knife stab at the face! get your thumb banged instead! counter with a dagger in the chest at the height of the scapula. The Hermaphrodite was not dead. Help! help! someone's coming . . . some men, how do I know? my mother! and once again I can see the room of the inn that had no locks on the doors: there were hooks, thank God, but how shrewd is the hermaphrodite: a hole in the attic, the stirring of a white shutter and the hermaphrodite comes down that way.

48 Grievous Last Appeal to the Phantoms Inspirers from the Past   I was born near a racetrack where I saw horses running beneath the trees. Oh! my trees! Oh! my horses! because all that existed for my sake. I was born near a racetrack! my childhood traced my name in the bark of the chest-

nut trees and the bushes! alas! my trees are no longer anything but the white feathers of a bird crying: "Leon! Leon!" Oh! diffuse memories of sumptuous chestnut trees where, as a child, I inscribed the name of my grandfather! Diffuse memories of races! jockeys! they are no longer anything but the pitiful toys they would appear from afar! the horses are no longer noble and the helmets of my jockeys are black. Come along, turn away! turn away! from old imprisoned thoughts that never will soar! the symbol that suits you is not the elastic gallop of jockeys on the green but some dusty bas-relief concealing from my grief the autumnal chestnut trees where the name of my grandfather is written.

Indexes

Index of Poems Cited

155

Index

DESIGNED BY GARY GORE
COMPOSED BY GRAPHIC COMPOSITION, INC., ATHENS, GEORGIA
MANUFACTURED BY CUSHING MALLOY, INC., ANN ARBOR, MICHIGAN
TEXT AND DISPLAY LINES ARE SET IN BASKERVILLE

Library of Congress Cataloging in Publication Data
Lévy, Sydney, 1943–
The play of the text.
Includes bibliographical references and indexes.
1. Jacob, Max, 1876–1944. Le cornet à dés.
I. Jacob, Max, 1876–1944. Le cornet à dés.
II. Title.
PQ2619.A17C6234   841′.912   80–52298
ISBN 0-299-08510-4   AACR2

DATE DUE